NEW MEMBERS = NEW GROWTH
It's up to you how you nurture them.

*"If God waited on people to become perfect
before He anointed them
to preach, teach, lead or minister,
there would never be anyone worthy,
and the work would never get done.*

*God uses willing vessels, with weaknesses,
so His strength, power, and anointing,
can shine through,
and He can get the glory!"*

Keith Hammond

Welcome To Our Church

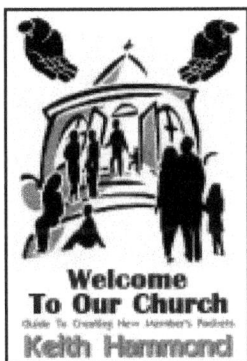

Guide To Creating New Member Packets

Cover Layout and Interior Design: Keith Hammond

Lessons For Life Books

PUBLISHERS

LESSONSFORLIFEBOOKS.COM

LessonsForLifeBooks.com

IMPRINT A Lessons For Life Book

Welcome To Our Church
Guide To Creating
New Member Packets

© 2012 by
Keith Hammond
is published by
Lessons for Life Books, Inc.
7455 France Ave. S. #305
Edina, MN 55435

ISBN-13: 978-1-938588-66-2
Library of Congress Control Number: 2012915258
Printed in the U.S.A.

Dedication

God Almighty,
I give you all the glory, honor, and praise for all that you have done
and still do in, to, and through, my life.
Thank you for Jesus Christ and the Holy Spirit,
and for the redeeming power of your Love.

To my wife,
in this 28th year together,
thank you for all your prayers and patience.

To my daughters,
my Love for you goes beyond words.
Many blessings to you both.

To my grandsons,
it is a great joy
to be Blessed with your presence in our lives.

To the Hammond and Fitzpatrick families,
I pray that you will unite arm in arm one day
and allow yourselves to be encircled by
the healing power of God's Love.

To Pastor Arthur Agnew,
only God could know how grateful I am,
for the 10 years you stood by my side.
Your training and teaching and telling will always be with me.

Acknowledgement

Ken E. at MMS,
I thank God for using you to be the springboard
that helped launch this ministry.
Thank you for the open door.
I'm forever grateful.

Dana Lynn Smith
The Savvy Book Marketer
Your wisdom, knowledge & understanding,
are incredible and inspiring.
Thank you for being my coach.

There are others who at some point and time of my life,
made a measurable impact, whether good or bad,
I am thankful for your input into me,
as it helped God prune, grow and mature me in more ways,
than you will ever know.

God Bless You All.

T O C

How Important Are New Members?

Before you answer this question, you need to first see, know and recognize that new members to your church are also existing members of their own family. This is important because they may have children to bring with them, or other friends and family. If you lose the first one, you've probably lost them all. Hopefully, this helps you see just how important your new members are.

New Members = New Growth

This should be a direct and distinct sign that your church is still connected to the Vine, is still a branch, has not been cut off, is still being pruned, and is considered a vital part of the Body of Christ. You have been entrusted with another soul to help get ready for Salvation. And your role in this is much more important than just having them fill out an index card with their name and address so you can add them to your database or mailing list or say they joined.

The new member that just entrusted their life to you, has been drawn by Jesus to a place where they now find themselves in front of God's messenger, the preacher. What Jesus used to draw them is not important, even if they tell you. What is important is what you do with this individual who has openly expressed their need for Salvation, their hope for change, and their desire to have a relationship with God, through our Lord and Savior Jesus Christ.

The moment they are in right now is quite possibly the most vulnerable they have been or will ever be. It is their new birth. They are infants all over again. And it is up to you to nurture them, feed them, lead them, guide them, direct them, train them, teach them, preach to them, rebuke them, correct them, forgive them and love them.

Because of every new member's importance to the growth of the church (I didn't say 'your' church, I said 'The' church) take the first step: Establish a New Members Ministry. Give them the task of creating the new member packet, which will also be used as the curriculum for the new member class. You'll see why as you read on.

New members should be welcomed to God's Family and His Kingdom with open, loving, non-judgemental arms, as if it were their first day of Kindergarten. They are probably joining 'your' church looking for God, but not yet know Jesus Christ or the Holy Spirit. So it is vitally important, and your eternal responsibility to help each new member learn the difference between 'your' church, and 'The' church. If you don't know what I just said, let me explain it to you.

Your church is the one 'you' started or pastor. 'The' church is the one Jesus founded. There is a 'measurable' difference. Your church is local, exists in the city you're in, operates from Earth to Heaven, etc. Jesus' church is global, exists from Heaven to Earth, etc.

Your church is the one where you turn the key in the door, turn the lights on, etc. Jesus's church has keys that fit another door, and is lit by power that needs no switches or outlets to turn on. Hopefully you get difference between 'your' church and 'The' church.

New Members = New Growth & New Growth = Kingdom Growth

New members are nervous. They are cautious. They are afraid. Here's a tip: People who recently arrived at the church as new members should never be given the responsibility of welcoming other new members. The responsibility of welcoming new members should be given to seasoned members with warmth, maturity, and who know a lot more about the church than another new member.

New Members Class

New members should be required to take a 'New Members Class' to learn about the church they've joined. The class should be taught by someone familiar with and active in every aspect of the church. It should be taught by someone in church leadership.

New Members Curriculum

The curriculum for a New Members Class should come directly from a compilation of material most important to helping new members adjust to their new life in Christ. It should contain 'both' a history of 'The' church, from the first altar built for worship (by Abel) in the Old Testament, through the building of the Tabernacle, to the Ministry of Jesus in the Gospel and up to the founding of 'The' church in the New Testament. Including the growth of Christianity and the planting of early churches by the Apostles, etc.

This is basic information that should be fed and taught to every New Member, so they can become acquainted with their role in both your church and The church and helped to remove certain worldly myths if they exist in their thoughts such as:

The Pastor is who I pay Tithes to.   [myth]
Tithes are due to, paid to, and in honor of God.   [fact]

Example Description: Under the Old Covenant, people did pay Tithes to the Priests. God discarded this process because the Priests became wicked, selfish, and stole from God by taking the Best of the sacrifices the people offered to God for absolution and forgiveness of their sins, keeping the Best for themselves as Priests, and substituting the sacrifice with Blind and Lame animals. God became angered at this, and started a New Covenant, by having the people bring all the Tithes to the (storehouse) church, not the Priests.

THE IMPORTANCE

New Members Packet

'Your Church'

New members should be given a 'New Members Packet' that contains information on 'Your Church' such as:

Your History
Your Pastor
Your Leadership
Your Mission
Your Services
Your Covenant
Your Beliefs
Your Auxiliaries
Your Membership
Your Tithing
Your Baptism
Your Communion
Your Sunday School
Your Bible Study
Your Vacation Bible School
Your Weddings
Your Funerals
Your Dedications
Your Youth
Your Choirs
Your Website
Your Newsletters
Your Television Outreach
Your Vision
Your Needs
Your Mission Work
Your Transportation
etc.

New Members Packet
'The Church'
In addition to the information about your church, every new member should be taught and or reminded of the very distinct difference between your church and The Church. Include info such as:
First Altar
First Tithe
First Conflict About Tithing
First Priests
First Sanctuary (Tabernacle)
First Covenant
First Commandments
The Ministry of Jesus &
The Foundation of The Church
The purpose is to show each new member the differences as well as the similarities between your church and The Church. And, how they work together as earthly preparation in your church for eternal worship as a member of The Church.

THE DESIGN

The overall **design** of your New Member Packet should reflect how much you care about new members.

Reminder: New members are NOT about 'your' church. They are new members of The Church, being ushered in via 'your' church.

The design of your New Member Packet should reflect God, Jesus and the Holy Spirit in each and every way. If your New Member Packet is:

- Designed or put together haphazardly
- Contains spelling errors
- Includes blurry photos & graphics
- Pages where the copier toner was low
- Coffee spilled on it
- Pages are out of order
- Stapled on the wrong side

Side Note: "Yes", I have seen each of these things on the New Member Packets of many churches.

...or anything that shows you didn't put care into it, start over, use a template, or call a pro.

Can't afford a pro?
ASK A MEMBER!
Don't have anyone capable or willing to take on the task?
PRAY FOR GOD'S DIRECTION!

Again, once you assign the task to a New Member Ministry, have that team develop or follow through on guidelines that you as the pastor, or the applicable governing authority have set forth. Honestly, you cannot afford not to have it professionally done, either by a member, or non-member professional. However, to assist you, at the end of this book, I've included a 40-page template for you to use as a sample and guide for your own Packet. VOILA!

Section One
The Content

History

Your New Member Packet should contain information on the history of your church. Such as:
• Who founded it
• What major events have happened since it was founded
• When was it founded
• Where was it founded
• Why was it founded
• How was it founded

Using the FIVE W's, throughout the entire process of creating your New Member Packet, you should be able to easily answer the questions set before you to come up with the content needed to complete the project. Remember, it's not about 'your church'. Your task is to help new members see how they fit into 'The Church' through your church.

History Tip:
It has been said that pictures are worth a thousand words. If that's true, then how much is a video?

In your History section, have your elder members gather up any and all the pictures & video from every church function as far back as they can go.

This will give you plenty of content needed.

Your New Member Packet should include a list of all the previous pastors is there are any, and a history of the leadership teams, their roles, etc. You should list and explain any past pastoral changes, new buildings, new projects such as if you built a school, etc.

The data in your history should reflect:
• Your past
• Your present
• Your future
All of this is important for new members to see where you came from, where you are now, and where you plan to go in the future. Again, including pictures is vital.

Pastor

This will probably be the most read page in the entire New Member Packet. The new member wants to know who it is they are placing their lives and possibly the lives of their family, in the hands of. Your pastor's bio should contain where he/she came from, who their family is, where they live, where they went to school, how they came to pastor the church, why they came to the city you're in and how long they've been there. It should also contain any major accomplishments in their life, both secular and in church. Again, using the FIVE W's, tell the new members:

• Who the pastor is
• What they've done in their life
• When did they start pastoring
• Where were they before coming to your church
• Why did they start pastoring
• How they came to your church

Your New Member Packet should include information on the Pastor's spouse and children. A short bio and picture can help new members identify them when they see and meet them, and reading their bio can help show that they are people with problems just like them.

The data in your Pastor section should reflect:
• His/Her past
• His/Her present
• His/Her future
All of this is important for new members to see where the pastor came from, where they are now, and where they plan taking the church in the future. Again, including pictures is vital.

Pastor Tip:
As part of the New Members Packet, you should include a personal letter from the pastor. It should reflect a welcome as well as personal insight from the Man or Woman of God as the servant leader of your church. New members often come to church because they see Jesus being reflected in the pastor by they way they preach or live their life.

Leadership

Your New Member Packet should contain information on who the overseers of your various church and ministry functions are. Such as:
• Who is the Leadership
• What area(s) are they responsible for
• When do they meet
• Where do they meet
• Why is your Leadership so (large/small)
• How do new members contact them (phone, email?)

Using the FIVE W's, show new members who's responsible for certain areas of the church. Such as who are the associate ministers, the deacons, deaconesses, and trustees. Who are the chairpersons of the auxiliaries such as ushers, choir, youth? Use pictures when possible. If you have a regular leadership meeting, include the schedule.

Leaders Tip:
New Members may have gifts they want to use in certain areas of the church such as the choir; or they may be interested in serving as ushers, etc. Give them the tools necessary to do that, and help them understand from a Biblical viewpoint, why such positions are important to both your church and to The Church. Every bit of info helps.

And, let the new members know when leadership changes take place such as elections, whether its every year or every two. Also, let them know if the meetings are public. And, let them know if you have protocol for applying for the positions in place.

The data in the Leaders section should reflect:
• Leadership past
• Leadership present
• Leadership future (vision, focus, plans, etc).
All of this is important for new members to see where you came from, where you are now, and where you plan to go in the future. Again, including pictures is vital.

Mission

Your mission statement will identify you to anyone who reads the New Member Packet. It should be a one page articulation of the way you see yourself in a few bullet points, a summation of your calling, a glimpse into your strategy, an introduction to your beliefs, your understanding of their situations, your encouragement to them to look to Jesus Christ for their salvation, a view of your purpose, and an invitation to them to participate in the New Member Class. Again, using the FIVE W's, tell new members:

• Who is responsible for the mission
• What the mission is
• When did the mission start
• Where is the mission displayed
• Why is the mission what it is
• How they play a part in the mission

Your mission statement should include very detailed descriptions using basic language so that new members can understand what your mission is as a church, but more importantly, how and why they are important to God, Jesus and the Holy Spirit as part of The Church.

The data in the Mission section should reflect:
• Mission past
• Mission present
• Mission future
All of this is important for new members to see where your mission came from, where it is now, and where the church is headed in the future. Again, including pictures is vital.

Mission Tip:
Your mission is as vital to new members, as it is to you. Why? Because our societal mindset, and our perceptions have most if not all humans thinking that every company, every nonprofit, every church, has a mission statement. So it is important to 'feed' that expected viewpoint with accurate information rather than letting them believe something else.

Services

Your New Member Packet should feature your regular worship services in a way that stands out from the rest of the material. Include:
• Who is in charge of different services (ex. men's night, women's night)
• What takes place during the worship (ex. Order of Service)
• When are they scheduled
• Where are they held
• Why services happen when they do (ex. annual, 5th Sunday, etc.)
• How do new members participate

Using the FIVE W's, you should prepare, if you don't have already, a list of your regular worship services and a list of your annual programs. This will be an opportunity for the New Member to see if you are truly serving God or if you are holding program after program after program to honor age-old traditions, and to raise funds to pay bills.

Services Tip:
Growth in a church is mandatory and there is plenty of Scripture to back up that statement. If you've been in existence for 10 years, but your growth has only been one new member added to your roster each month over the entire time, your New Member Auxiliary should focus on Evangelism in addition to designing a New Member Packet.

In my humble opinion, church should no longer be done the way it has been in the past of holding programs and services to follow traditions. Fewer people are joining churches that are following tradition, and more people are looking desperately for God's Way, and His Truth.

The Services section should reflect:
• Services past
• Services present
• Services future
This is important for new members to see how the church has grown over time. I'm one who thinks new believers should avoid churches with no growth. Again, pictures are vital.

Covenant

While many church covenants come from age-old tradition, yours should speak to the Biblical truth of how and why you exist as a church. It should tell new members that a covenant is an agreement between them and God; it is a promise God makes to them, that He keeps; a written document many churches operate by; an arrangement they should always honor; and a promise from God that He honors. Again, using the FIVE W's, tell the new members:
• Who wrote, developed, adopted your covenant
• What the covenant is
• When did the covenant come into begin
• Where is the covenant displayed
• Why the covenant is written the way it is
• How they play a part in the covenant

Your church covenant section should include a very detailed description using basic language so that new members can understand what your covenant is, but more importantly, how and why covenants are important to God, Jesus and the Holy Spirit as part of The Church.

The Covenant section should reflect:
• Covenant past
• Covenant present
• Covenant future
All of this is important for new members to see where your covenant came from, where it is now, and where the church is headed covenantly, in the future.

Covenant Tip:
Is your church covenant proudly display in your lobby, bulletins, brochure, anywhere? Where can new members locate info about your covenant and the differences between the covenant that governs your church, and any and all Covenants God made, and continues to honor since the early days of humanity. Having this info available is vital to clarity.

Beliefs

Your Beliefs are what shows new members how and where you're sticking to Biblical principals rather than adopting worldly views. Include:
• Who established your core beliefs
• What (if not the Bible) is the basis for the belief(s)
• When (if ever) are they reviewed
• Where are they displayed
• Why (if they are) do they differ from Biblical teachings
• How do new members share their views

Using the FIVE W's, here's where you shine! This doc should promote how you see the God, His Son Jesus Christ, the Holy Spirit and the Trinity. Your belief statement should also be summary of your core values, goals, milestone markers, collaboration principles, improvement plan, strategies, key results indicators and performance measures.

Beliefs Tip:
If your church supports gay union, you will most likely lose new members who believe the sanctity of marriage was created by God as a covenant between Him, one man and one woman. Let new members know, up front, what your core beliefs are so they can make decisions about their walk with Christ and their membership in your church.

It should show the new member your organizational structure, framework, the building blocks for your improvement, accountability, and future goals. It should give them a sense that you're not only a church, but you understand what it means to operate a business.

The Beliefs section should reflect:
• Beliefs past
• Beliefs present
• Beliefs future
This is important for new members to see how the church has been molded and shaped by God over time. Use generic pictures in this section, and focus on textual quality.

Ministry

This section sets you apart from every other church on the planet, and helps new members see why you're different. If you are a church steeped in tradition, aren't adapting to an ever-changing society, you most likely don't have components in place to handle the list of problems new members face such as drug/alcohol addiction, debt elimination, abstinence, teen pregnancy, homelessness, absentee/incarcerated parents, and a wide variety of other issues, on top of ministries that feed the hungry, visit the sick, etc. Again, using the FIVE W's, tell the new members:

• Who is in charge of your various ministries
• What the list of ministries are
• When did each ministry start
• Where are ministry meetings held
• Why the ministry was created (ex. to feed people in your community)
• How they can get involved in the various ministries

If your church isn't doing anything but praying to help your members get through the many struggles, challenges and temptations they'll begin to see surface once they've given their lives to Christ, this section won't impress any new member who is truly seeking growth.

The Ministry section should reflect:
• Ministries past
• Ministries present
• Ministries future
All of this is VITAL for new members to see where your Ministry focus was, where it is now, and where the church sees it can impact the lives of others in the future.

Ministry Tip:
Many churches today do nothing to help feed the hungry, clothe the naked, visit the sick, minister to prisoners, help strangers, or even take care of widows and orphans. Churches like this are identified and warned in Matthew 25:31-46 and James 2:14-16. New members should see the compassion of Jesus working in you, in this section.

Membership

Your Beliefs are what shows new members how and where you're sticking to Biblical principals rather than adopting worldly views. Include:
• Who are your current members
• What are current members involved in at church
• When do the members meet amongst themselves
• Where can they get more info on current members
• Why can't new members do things that seasoned saints do
• How do new members share their views

Using the FIVE W's, tell new members if the church secretary or someone else maintains a roster of member information such as address, phone numbers, email addresses and names of family members. Any info on relocation, corrections, updates and changes to their general family structure and lifestyle such as weddings.

Members Tip:
This is a very helpful area for new members. By you including 'Member Testimonials' in your new member packet, it will give the newest members a chance to see and hear how your church has affected the lives of other since they've joined. It's also helpful to put a face with the testimonial. Your new member may know the person they see!

And, a database that keeps track of all the member information including pictures and pledges. Copies of the roster should be given to new members in their class so they can feel like they're part of your membership, now that they've joined your church.

The Members section should reflect:
• Members past
• Members present
• Member testimonials
This is important for new members to see how the church has affected the lives of others who have joined over time. Use pictures in this section, so new members can see who they are.

Tithes

How do you tell new members who just lost their home to foreclosure that they need to Tithe? You just do. You're obligated to preach the word, in season and out. Teach that Tithing takes place in their heart long before it ever comes from the firstfruits of income. It's scriptural; the primary part of their worship; and beneficial; It requires sacrifice. New members often come to church because they're facing an overwhelming problem or situation.

Again, using the FIVE W's, tell the new members:
• Who do the Tithes get paid to
• What is the Scripture mandating Tithing
• When do new members Tithe
• Where can new members learn more about Tithing
• Why is Tithing necessary
• How can new members be consistent Tithers

Before people become new members in any church, they often come to the church seeking help with any number of financial difficulties and they seek out the church for help because they have nowhere else to go. It's your responsibility to teach them that churches sometimes help members with certain things, but rarely money.

The Tithing section should reflect:
• Tithing past
• Tithing present
• Tithing future
This information is VITAL for new members to learn how God says His system of protection and provision works.

Tithing Tip:
Help new members learn and understand that their Tithes do not line the pockets of the pastor. Teach that Tithes is a mandate, is a requirement that God has placed upon all brothers and sisters in Christ, and they are not alone in the process of Tithing. Help them also learn how to teach their children these valued and valuable Godly principles of obedience.

Offering

Your offering section should help new members understand the very distinct differences between Tithing and Offering. Include:
• Who do offerings get paid to
• What Scriptures instruct and cover Offerings
• When should Offerings be given
• Where can new members get more information on Offering
• Why new members shouldn't just Tithe and skip giving Offering
• How do new members choose when to give Offerings

Using the FIVE W's, teach new members why it's important to not only Tithe, but to also stretch beyond their requirement to Title, and show God that they are a 'cheerful giver'. This section should explain that their offering is giving that starts in the heart. It should be because they've been blessed with more than they need so it can be used to help others. And it requires

Offering Tip:
I suggest giving new members a list of things that have been built, or created, or developed, as a direct result of offering from members. Show them how when they plant a seed, it starts the growth process for whatever it is they made the sacrifice to sow into. Help them to see that giving is a vital part of their worship, obedience, and membership.

Teach them that offerings are very often used and described as a way to 'plant or sow a seed' into your church or another ministry. And help them understand why sowing seeds is important to their own growth as well.

The Offering section should reflect:
• Offering past
• Offering present
• Offering testimonials or needs
This is important because it can help new members understand how things work in your church. Such as helping to support a needed ministry, or helping to give to a family that lost a home, or giving just because they see someone in need.

Baptism

Your Baptism should be a critical part of the new member process. It is how new members show their commitment to inward change. Include:
• Who is in charge of Baptisms
• What Scriptures instruct and cover Baptism
• When does your church Baptize new members
• Where can new members get more information on Baptism
• Why new members can't just skip getting Baptized
• How do new members prepare for Baptism

Using the FIVE W's, teach new members who have a hope to be baptized with water why it's important to also receive the baptism of the Holy Spirit. This is the place to show them that they need both. Make them aware of the process of preparing to be baptized, who will be contacting them with instructions, and what they will need, if anything, to be ready.

Let them know when baptisms take place, and where. And give them a sense of comfort in knowing the benefit of the outward sign showing inward change. Show them why every new member of the Body of Christ needs to be baptized.

The Baptism section should reflect:
• Baptisms past
• Baptisms present
• Baptism testimonials
This is important for new members to see how the process of Baptism has affected the lives of others who have joined over time. Use pictures in this section, so new members can see who stepped forward to be baptized.

Baptism Tip:
Be sure to explain the reasons for being baptized, the process of being baptized, the power of being baptized, the commitment it takes to be baptized, and the many other things associated with baptism. Take this opportunity to share with new members what being baptized with fire means as it relates to the Holy Spirit. Acts 2:38 is a great place to start this section.

Communion

Communion is critical to new members. It is the process used by the Body of Christ to remember, recall and review why Jesus died for our sins. Include:

• Who do we participate in communion
• What Scriptures instruct and cover Communion
• When should Communion be taken and when not
• Where can new members get more information on Communion
• Why new members should examine themselves before Communion
• How does Communion affect the life of a new member

Using the FIVE W's, teach new members about communion? If you conduct the ceremony the 1st Sunday of every month like most churches, new members need to know; If there's a specific procedure, new members need to know; If you use something other than grape juice and crackers, new members need to know.

Communion Tip:
Some churches host the communion ceremony once a month. Others, only on major holidays. Whatever your schedule, the same information about the reasons behind communion is just as vital whenever it's done. 'Do this in remembrance of me' is a direct command from Jesus to 'do' it as an act of worship to show Jesus that you will never forget His sacrifice.

Whatever your tradition is around Communion, new members will especially need to know the reason your church believes in the need for the ceremony. Explain the process start to finish, in complete detail in the packet.

The Communion section should reflect:
• Offering past
• Offering present
• Offering testimonials or needs
This is important because it can help new members understand how things work in your church. Such as helping to support a needed ministry, or helping to give to a family that lost a home, or giving just because they see someone in need.

Sunday School

Your Sunday School is another critical part of the new member process. It is where new members will be educated on their new walk with Christ. Include:
• Who is in charge of Sunday School
• What Scriptures cover Sunday School
• When does your church hold Sunday School
• Where can new members get more information on Sunday School
• Why new members need Sunday School
• How do new members grow in Sunday School

Using the FIVE W's, showcase how your Sunday School is a rowing and nurturing place for development of the Christian lifestyle. Tell new members what your focus is, such as teaching each student at their level of growth without pushing them too fast, while they're learning more about God, Jesus Christ and the Holy Spirit through the Bible and other tools.

Give new members the Sunday morning schedule and encourage them to bring others to Sunday school, even if they aren't members of your church. Sunday School (and Bible Study) are the only places new members can interact with other members in an informal setting.

The Sunday School section should reflect:
• Sunday School past
• Sunday School present
• Sunday School testimonials
This information is important because new members experience their first signs of growth in a Christian education setting. Help them to learn how vital it is to their maturity in Christ.

Sunday School Tip:
Be creative. Your new members may be someone else's old members. Help them fit in your church by giving them fresh, new and creative ways to seeing the Gospel of Jesus Christ from an Old and New Testament perspective, with skits, team-teaching, and plenty of graphics, quizzes and tests. Be mindful of auditory and visual learners.

Bible Study

Bible Study is the other critical part of Christian Education for new members. You must remember that new members may not be able to read, and may have never been in a structured classroom setting. Include:
• Who is in charge of Bible Study
• What Scriptures instruct and cover Bible Study
• When is Bible Study held
• Where can new members get more information on Bible Study
• Why new members should make a commitment to Bible Study
• How does Bible Study affect the life of a new member

Using the FIVE W's, let new members know when Bible study classes are. Also let them know if you take summer breaks for Vacation Bible School. Teach them that studying the Bible is the primary foundation for their growth in Christ; that there is a difference between 'study' and reading.

Bible Study Tip:
Use this opportunity to help new members learn about the importance and vitality of the Living, Active, Breathing, Two-Edged Sword that is God's Word. Teach them that the words on the pages are just from the Alphabet, but from the Alpha Himself. Show them that their lives will never be the same once they give themselves to studying God's Word.

If your Bible Study uses other tools for teaching such as my book 'Dictionary Of Bible Lessons', let new members know. Give them assurance that you realize that the Bible is and always will be the main source for the Word of God.

The Bible Study section should reflect:
• Bible Study past
• Bible Study present
• Bible Study future
This is important because it can help new members understand how your church uses the Bible for teaching and training. It can help new members learn and grow and mature in ways they never dreams because of the Living Word.

Other Training

Your other areas of Training are just as vital to new members as Bible Study and Sunday School. It brings richness and diversity in Christian education from another perspective. Include:
• Who is in charge of other Training
• What Scriptures cover other Training
• When does your church participate in other Training
• Where can new members get more information on other Training
• Why new members need other Training
• How do new members grow in other Training

Using the FIVE W's, promote and encourage new members (even if your church is steeped in tradition), to pursue other Training at other locations such as annual conventions, workshops, annual retreats, etc. Such other Training can provide valuable info and can be a healthy supplement.

Otherwise, where will they get exposure to other teaching methods such as skits and plays, guest speakers, hands-on activities, and other creative ways to help them further their walk with Christ and learn how to be leaders? Give them a list of classes you recommend locally, nationally and online.

The Other Training section should reflect:
• Other Training past
• Other Training present
• Other Training testimonials
This information is VITAL because it can help new members get experience on how Christians in other parts of the world learn and grow.

Other Training Tip:
As of 2012, I've served in two churches over 15 years. One church made other Training part of their Christian Education by taking the entire church to an annual convention with classes. I can't create a list long enough to show the benefits I've received from the classes. The other church, does not participate in any outside training as a Body.

Youth

It is VITAL to let new members know that your church takes an active roles in the lives of youth because of the vast amount of temptations in the world, and the opposition to their Christian lifestyle. Include:
- Who is in charge of the Youth Ministry
- What Scriptures instruct and cover Youth Ministry
- When are Youth Ministry meetings and activities held
- Where can new members get more information on Youth Ministry
- Why new members with kids should involve them in Youth Ministry
- How does Youth Ministry affect the life of a young new members

Using the FIVE W's, let new members know that you believe that "It takes a village to raise a child" because with society trying to take God out of our schools that your church does everything it can to counter that anti-Christian message with the truth of God's Word.

Youth Ministry Tip: Churches that do not take an active role in its youth, are doing a major disservice to the Body of Christ. I believe that the wisdom that comes from God with age, should be the ones helping to lead Youth Ministries, as part of the team. Pairing the older (senior) members of your church with youth will prove to be invaluable as an asset for growth.

Let them know if you have meetings, annual retreats, services, programs, training, outings and other activities for youth. Especially outside activities that teach them to serve others such as feeding the hungry, visiting the sick, etc.

The Youth Ministry section should reflect:
- Youth Ministry past
- Youth Ministry present
- Youth Ministry testimonials and future plans

This section can help adult new members gain a level of comfort in your church knowing that their kids are in good hands. More importantly, help them to see and know that with you, their kids are in God's hands. Use lots of pictures.

Choir

Is your Choir a growing group of dedicated, committed followers of Jesus Christ that use their gift of song, music and dance to worship and praise and give glory to God? In this section, include:
• Who is in charge of the various Choirs
• What Scriptures cover your Music Ministry
• When does the various Choirs meet
• Where can new members get more information on the Choirs
• Why new members should participate in the Choir
• How do new members grow by using their gifts in the Choir

Using the FIVE W's, let new members know if your choir produced any CDs. If your music ministry uses praise dancers. Who the chairpersons are. The names of the choirs. If you have audio/visual technicians or need some. This is one area that new members can feel part of your church.

You'll need to let new members know as much information about this section as you possibly can. Why? Because they may be gifts in music, dance or song. They may have children who are the same.

The Choir section should reflect:
• Choir past
• Choir present
• Choir testimonials and future plans
The relationships that are formed within a group such as a church choir can be lasting and stronger than most bonds. There are untold and immeasurable benefits from lifting ones voice to God in song. Use pictures in this area.

Choir Tip:
In 15 years of serving at two churches, I have seen no area with greater growth potential than the Choir. If a Choir, takes a single song, and shares it with the world over the many avenues of global media, Jesus Christ can be introduced, heard about, and lifted up locally, nationally, and internationally within a matter of days. That's powerful.

Visitors

How you treat your visitors often determines whether or not they will ever consider becoming members. Do you publicly welcome your visitors during the worship services? Do you publicly make them feel welcome? Include:
• Who is in charge of welcoming Visitors
• What Scriptures instruct and cover Visitors
• When are Visitors followed up with and how
• Where can new members get more information on Visitor protocol
• Why new members should help engage Visitors
• How does welcoming Visitors affect the growth of new members

Using the FIVE W's, explain to new members that you want every visitor to the House of God to feel welcome; that you give each visitor a welcome packet with information on the church, your pastor, services, mission, vision, auxiliaries, ministries, website, transportation and other items.

Visitors Tip:
I've served two churches over 15 years. Each one treated visitors differently. One, publicly had visitors to stand, be recognized, and allowed them time to speak. The other, nothing. A Visitor's experience at your church will either be positive or negative and either kept secret, or told to everyone they know. The reception you give = the response you get.

Teach new members that you understand the importance of Visitors, because they may one day become members. And new members bring a variety of gifts, skills, talents, abilities, memory, knowledge, understanding, and resources, able to help grow your church and ministry.

The Visitors section should reflect:
• Visitors past
• Visitors present
• Visitor testimonials
This section can help new members see how you treat them, as well as anyone that comes to the church on behalf of them. Use lots of pictures and testimonials in this area.

Weddings

These collaborations are always something special and letting new members know that your church believes in and honors the sanctity of the covenant of marriage is vital. In this section, include:
• Who is in charge of your wedding planning
• What Scriptures cover your Weddings
• When do coordinators meet and what do they charge
• Where can new members get more information on Weddings
• Why new members should use your church in planning their Wedding
• How do new members use their gifts to help with Weddings

Using the FIVE W's, let new members know that whether the space to host weddings is limited to just two, can hold two hundred or two thousand, let new members know that they will have a truly blessed experience that they will remember for the rest of their lives.

Teach new members that God is always the first in planning, and carrying out the event. Their wedding day should be something they can look forward to you allowing you to be a part of. Be sure to give them a list of options and contacts. They may feel less stressed when you're involved.

The Wedding section should reflect:
• Weddings past
• Weddings present
• Wedding testimonials
A Wedding can be one of the most important and the most memorable experiences of your new members. Use lots and lots of pictures and video in this area.

Weddings Tip:
I've seen and participated in Weddings for other members, and even with one of my own daughters. Nothing is more sacred and more important to a new member who looks to their church to help plan, support, and carry out their Wedding. But if it isn't done right, it can be one of the most stressful experiences. Again, if not done Godly and properly,

Funerals

Loss has been a part of my life since childhood. From 1970 to 1980 I suffered through the loss of my mom, dad, many other relatives, as well as two best friends. Support the family during this time. Include:
- Who is in charge of coordinating Funerals
- What Scriptures instruct and cover Funerals
- When are Funerals conducted
- Where can new members get more information on Funeral protocol
- Why new members should be knowledgeable about Funerals
- How do Funerals affect new members

Using the FIVE W's, let new members know that you understand the loss of a loved one is a tremendous strain on any family. It most often comes at a time when we least expect it. And, hardly anyone ever plans for it. Let new members know that your church can help.

Funeral Tip:
As I edit this book and prepare to upload and make it available online, I'm reeling at the loss of a nephew just on yesterday. He was 26 years old, and passed away suddenly of a heart attack. Without the church involved in this time of grieving, a family feels the loss greater than if they had support from many prayers and sources.

Let them know that you're available to help with just about anything they'll need during this time of transition. Let them know you're available at any time day or night to answer questions or provide any support they might need. Let them know if you're able to design the programs and handle most of the logistics. It'll ease their mind.

The Funerals section should reflect:
- Funerals past
- Funerals present
- Funeral testimonials
This section can help new members see how you families in crisis. And how you govern and respond in this area has lasting impact.

Dedications

New births are always an exciting time for new parents. I've been in churches where babies couldn't be dedicated unless they were from married couples. If that's your policy, let new members know it. Include:

• Who is in charge of your Dedications and Christenings
• What Scriptures cover your Dedications and Christenings
• When do coordinators meet and what is the protocol
• Where can new members learn more about Dedications & Christenings
• Why new members should use your church in planning their Dedication
• How do new members use their gifts to help with Dedications

Using the FIVE W's, teach new members that Proverbs says, "Children are a gift from God." Let them know if that's why you believe that they should be dedicated back to God. List what you'll provide, help prepare, plan and make post Dedication decisions.

Knowing that you care about the new member of the new member will help in more ways that you can count, list, or imagine. I've witnessed new births bring renewed believe in God. I've seen new parents with no prior belief in God all of a sudden begin to have Faith. I've seen new dads, want to change their life instantly.

The Wedding section should reflect:
• Weddings past
• Weddings present
• Wedding testimonials
A Dedication or Christening can be one of the most important and the most memorable to new members. Use lots and lots of pictures.

Dedications Tip:
This is another area where the more that you can help new members understand your beliefs and values and protocol concerning this Blessed event, the better. Mostly all parents believe their child is a Blessing from God. But if your church won't dedicate the child of an unmarried couple back to God, you want new members to know right away.

Website

The Internet is the place where most people get their information. They will bypass several TVs, remote controls, newspapers and books to get to the computer and the World Wide Web. Include:

• Who is in charge of your church Website
• What does your Website contain that's helpful to new members
• When is the Website updated
• Where can new members get more information on the Website
• Why new members should be knowledgeable about the Website
• How does the Website include or affect new members

Using the FIVE W's, teach that although the word "web" suggests a trap, if your church doesn't have its own website, blog, social media page, and access to sermons via audio, video, and other methods, you may not only lose new members, but find it very difficult speaking life into their lives.

Website Tip:
So many churches these days are directing people 'away' from their own website, and encouraging people to 'follow' them to a social media page. What's wrong with your site? Why on Earth would you promote someone else's site over your own? Do not send new members to another site to be fed who knows what, if your site meets the need.

Let new members know that your website address should be memorized so they can begin to share the location of the site with other people they meet. Help new members understand the importance of your church staying active in the areas of providing sermons via many methods so you can potentially reach the masses globally.

The Website section should reflect:
• Website past
• Website present
• Website testimonials and future plans
This section can help new members see how you connect with others across the globe.

Newsletter

Churches should publish a newsletter that's distributed to your immediate community. It gives new members insight into upcoming events, schedules, social issues, and a place for the Pastor to share his views. Include:
• Who is in charge of your Newsletter
• What Scriptures cover your Newsletter
• When do writers, editors, designers, columnists, etc., meet
• Where can new members get more information on the Newsletter
• Why new members should share their testimony in the Newsletter
• How do new members use their gifts to help with the Newsletter

Using the FIVE W's, I also suggest each Ministry to include their info to share employment opportunities, housing referrals, meeting locations, and a place for the congregation and new members to share their views. People are looking for churches that are preaching raw uncut truth.

Teach them, and your new members, that your church does not compromise God's Word to keep members who want to support gay unions, and other anti-Christian behavior. And let them know that the word that's preached into their hearing is God's Word, and not a one Scripture sermon given by man's interpretation and performance.

The Newsletter section should reflect:
• Newsletters past
• Newsletters present
• Newsletter testimonials and future plans
A Newsletter can be one of the best ways to share what you're doing with new members.

Newsletter Tip:
Over 15 years, I've served two churches. Neither published a newsletter. Neither was active in the community. One didn't even know the neighbors. The other, knew 'some' neighbors and made attempts to interact with the community. But without a newsletter or a postcard with a website url, neighbors a block away didn't know the church existed.

Television

Television is still one of the best methods to spread the Good News of the Gospel all over your community, your city, your state, and your country. Cable TV and Internet have driven broadcasting costs way down. Include:
• Who is in charge of your church TV Outreach
• What does your TV Show contain that's helpful to new members
• When is the TV Show updated
• Where can new members get more information on the TV Show
• Why new members should be knowledgeable about the TV Show
• How does the TV Show include or affect new members

Using the FIVE W's, teach new members that you're actively working to spread the Gospel worldwide to reach those who can't make it to church; are unfamiliar with church; don't know Jesus; haven't accepted Jesus as their Lord and Savior; or are looking for a loving church home.

TV Outreach Tip:
Of the two churches I've served in, one has a 125 year history, but has never aired a single TV commercial. The other, has a very active weekly one-hour broadcast on five different cable access networks across many cities. However your church does it, this is a truly dynamic way to reach people who have no idea you or Jesus exists.

You may reach new members with a sermon, choir, discussions about poverty, race, crime, drugs, domestic violence, divorce, and other issues they face daily. Help new members understand the importance of your church staying active in the areas of providing sermons via many methods so you can potentially reach the masses globally.

The Television section should reflect:
• TV Outreach past
• TV Outreach present
• TV Outreach testimonials and future plans
This section can help new members see how you connect with others across the globe.

Vision

What is your vision for the future of your church? Do you need a new building? Are you already building one? Are you buying a mall to provide jobs? Whatever your vision, share it with your new members. Include:
• Who is helping to manifest your Vision
• What Scriptures cover your Vision
• When does the committee covering the Vision meet
• Where can new members get more information on the Vision
• Why new members should be knowledgeable of the Vision
• How do new members use their gifts to help with the Vision

Using the FIVE W's, let them know if you need more space to seat more people and to accommodate people with disabilities; let them know if it has become more difficult for your elder members to attend services. However you convey the message of your vision, do it.

Add visuals and "overfeed" them with information. Vision is Vitally important to God. It's so important that God uses it in many Scriptures in the Bible such as: 'sits high and looks low'. The place and purpose you were, are, and plan to go, should be shown to new members in every possible way. It should be easy for them to see, read, take in, and share with others.

The Vision section should reflect:
• Vision past
• Vision present
• Vision testimonials and future plans
Your Vision can help new members learn how to get on board with where God is taking you.

Vision Tip:
There are three types of Vision...
• God's Vision
• Your Vision
• World Vision
Each of these Visions is Vitally important to your growth and success. God's Vision is Alpha; Your Vision is Anointed; the World Vision is Anti-Christ, and is where Alpha & Anointed do battle for new member's souls.

Needs

Your vision and your needs may interconnect at some point. In fact, your needs may precipitate the reason for the vision. God's Vision is for us to prosper in every aspect of our lives where HE is lifted up first. Include:

• Who is in charge of your Needs List
• What does your Needs List contain that's helpful to new members
• When is the Needs List updated
• Where can new members get more information on the Needs List
• Why new members should be knowledgeable about the Needs List
• How does the Needs List include or affect new members

Using the FIVE W's, teach new members that you're actively working to meet the needs of others and that they can help by just taking one item on the Needs List and praying and focusing their efforts on that one item. After a while, you can check that item off and start to work on another.

Needs List Tip:
My suggestion to you is to do three lists:
1. Basic Items
Things you always need.
2. Bigger Items
Items costing more to get.
3. Broadest Items
Things it will take one or more fundraisers to get. Each of these lists will help show new members where you are, what you need, and where you're trying to go and why.

What does a Need List look like? If you have makeshift classrooms; only two offices (for Pastor and Secretary); an audio room that doubles as a something else; your kitchen's being used as a classroom; both the men and women's bathrooms have only two stalls each; and the Baptismal pool is old or you don't have one, let new members know. You never know what kind of resources they may have to help.

The Needs List section should reflect:
• Needs List past
• Needs List present
• Needs List testimonials and future plans
This is how new members can feel needed.

Mission

Is your church active in International ministry 'at home'? Do you even understand what this means? Let me explain. There are many people from other cultures living near your church. How do you reach them? Include:
• Who is responsible for Mission work
• What Scriptures cover your Mission
• When does the committee covering Mission Work meet
• Where can new members get more information on the Mission
• Why new members should be knowledgeable of the Mission
• How do new members use their gifts to help with the Mission

Using the FIVE W's, teach new members that you're actively involved in spreading the Gospel to 'all nations'. Many churches have no idea how. The easiest way to reach people in other cultures is to put an anointed person from that culture in charge of the Mission to reach out to that culture.

If no one in your church speaks the language of the people you're trying to reach, you need someone that does. If your church can't translate God's Word into Bibles in the language of that culture, you need someone that can. The easiest way to get started is to ask God to order your steps to the right person, and give them the charge to head up that Mission Work.

The Mission section should reflect:
• Mission past
• Mission present
• Mission testimonials and future plans
Your Mission can help new members learn how you reach out to other cultures globally.

Mission Tip:
Take a class, take your church on a mission trip, if you can't afford to travel to another country, take a trip, in your city, to the nearest community that is filled with people from another country and culture. Remember, it's not about you. It's about doing all you can, while you can, to help spread the Gospel of Jesus Christ to all nations. So get to work.

Transportation

If your church gives rides to church services and other church functions new members may certainly think that's important. Let them know who to contact and what the process is. Include:

- Who is in charge of Transportation to and from church
- What is the policy and protocol for getting help with Transportation
- When are the Transportation meetings held for feedback
- Where can new members get more information on Transportation
- Why new members should be knowledgeable about Transportation
- How does the Transportation include or affect New Members

Using the FIVE W's, teach new members how to get on the list for rides. If you don't have a policy in place, set one. Make sure any message you send is consistent and always enforced. If you provide transportation to other places, such as annual church trips, let them know that as well.

Transportation Tip: 15 years, two churches. One was proactive and purchased a van years ago to help members in need get to church. The other, pastor and his wife are the taxicab. New members need to know that you care more about them getting to church to hear God's Word, than you do what people think about your sacrifice to get them to church.

If they need it, they'll be glad you did. Why? Simple. Imagine being a member of your church and you're an elderly person who can no longer drive, but no one has offered to help you get to church. Or, imagine being a single woman with several children, and no car, and no one even pays attention how you get to church. Or, imagine being physically challenged, and the only way to get to church is if someone brings you.

The Transportation section should reflect:
- Transportation past
- Transportation present
- Transportation testimonials and future plans
This is how new members can feel included.

Meetings

Do you publish a list of meetings that occur regularly? Whoever is in charge of the New Member's Ministry should send out invitations to get involved to all new members who are not active yet. Include:
• Who is responsible for the various Meetings
• What Scriptures cover what you're Meeting about
• When does the committee involving New Members meet
• Where can new members get more information on the Meetings
• Why new members should be knowledgeable of the Meetings
• How do the Meetings include or affect New Members

Using the FIVE W's, set the precedent for new members to expect to receive regular reminders of upcoming Meetings. It lets them know you're not only thinking about them, but you are aware that they are a member of your church and you are seeking their involvement in some small way.

I've been to churches that think all they're supposed to do is meet about any and everything. But there is rarely little progress or growth. Churches that need support in certain areas must have Meetings to plan and assign action items, but the follow-through is vitally more important than the Meeting. And, if you're only Meeting about 'internal' programs & services, you're missing the point of the Meeting.

The Meetings section should reflect:
• Meetings past
• Meetings present
• Meetings future
This is one way new members measure growth.

Meetings Tip:
Ok, so you're a small church. But you have members that have been there a decade. And they're committed. But the leadership in this area of Meeting to just plan 'internal' programs & services is lacking. Give your leadership the assignment based on your Vision, and let them help you make it happen. To do it, you have to release it.

Neighborhood

Does your community have a neighborhood group? One way to get new members involved in your church and in your community is to train them to get involved in the neighborhood group. Include:
• Who is in charge of the Neighborhood Group
• What is the procedure for joining the Neighborhood Group
• When are the Neighborhood meetings held
• Where can new members get more information on the Neighborhood
• Why new members should be knowledgeable about the Neighborhood
• How does the Neighborhood include or affect New Members

Using the FIVE W's, teach new members how to get information on the history of the community, the people, resources, and any help available to your church. This is a good new member project because it includes them, and lets them know you trust them to represent the church.

Neighborhood Tip:
The first church I served at, for 7 of the 12 years, I was actively involved in the Neighborhood Group. It was a great way to stay on top of things that could affect the church. The second church, doesn't even know its neighbors. As a business owner, I became a member of the Chamber of Commerce to stay on top of issues that could affect our church.

Neighborhood Groups are VITAL to your church especially if you're in the inner city. These groups have government authority to plan and fund and act out certain things. And, they have a direct relationship to the elected official for your community. Thus, including yourself in the process, by bringing a Godly source to the table, with a direct relationship to God, can have tremendous impact on your community.

The Neighborhood section should reflect:
• Neighborhood Group past
• Neighborhood Group present
• Neighborhood testimonials and future plans
This is how new members can feel included.

Section Two
The Commitment

THE DIRECTION

The **direction** your New Member Packet takes is determined by the content you put in it. Everything in it must be from spirit and truth. It's your church's resume, but there is no need for embellishments. It's important to view the packet as an anthology, and an opportunity to show strangers who you are as a church.

THE DECISION

The **decision**-making process of what goes into each element of your New Member Packet should be a collaborative effort. You should ask the head of each Ministry to provide input in the form of a one-page summary of their cause, their efforts, their needs. The input should be all on one accord.

THE DEDICATION

The **dedication** to completing your New Member Packet must be a priority. With these bleak economic times, New Members need to know that because of the sacrifice Jesus made on the cross, it gave Christians "access" to having all their needs supplied by God's riches in glory, and that we are recession proof!

THE DECLARATION

The **declaration** to your members is vital. Let them know you are taking this step to ensure that potential new members know you are committed to growing your membership through their input and involvement. And that creating this New Member Packet is the first step to achieving that goal.

THE DENOMINATION

The **denomination** you promote will have a broad effect on whether you attract new members or repel them. In today's society, many churches are founded based on 'denomination', rather than being followers of Jesus Christ. Don't promote their denomination more than The One who created it. Be mindful.

Reminder: You can find more books like this on
L e s s o n s F o r L i f e B o o k s . c o m

THE DETERMINATION

The **determination** to make your focus on new members a core part of the foundation of your church will need to be a "buy-in" from all stakeholders including current members of the congregation, the pastoral staff, church officers, and the community. Your approach to this will be evident in how determined you are to make that happen.

THE DEVELOPMENT

The **development** of the New Member Packet is just one component of a New Member Ministry. Without new members, you church will never grow, and will most likely eventually cease to operate. New members are the continued life-blood of every church, and when they stop coming, you should be very worried.

THE DISTRIBUTION

The **distribution** of information relative to your church is vital. Whichever form you are most comfortable with, you will settle into. However, settling into things often makes for a passive church and being passive is not always the best way to attract new members.

THE DEPOSIT

In order to get anything to grow, you must first plant the seed, someone must water it, then God will give increase. The **deposit** you make into new members today, will pay off with interest in the future. If you involve them in your meetings, get their input on programs and celebrations that honor God, and engage them in community discussions and forums, you will reap great rewards in the future, for the seeds you plant today.

THE DELIVERY

Now that you've read how to compile the information to begin the design and development of your New Members Packet, let's talk about the **delivery**.

The New Member's Ministry must be taught how and tasked where to get new members. If you're a traditional church with 95% of your members coming from outside of your immediate community, you may get angry at this next statement: "opening the doors of the church and waiting for people to join IS NOT considered the great commission, it's not even community outreach."

In the community where your church is located, if you don't know your neighbors, meaning every neighbor within a 4 block radius, your church is lacking in its community presence. What do you do about it? You can do several things, but you need to do them regularly and consistently in order to make the impact that every church needs to have in its own community. Your church needs to constantly be in the eyes and in the minds of the neighbors around you.

Here are some ideas:
1. Plan a neighborhood get together. Hosted at your church.
2. Create a one-page flyer and have members deliver it door to door.
3. Start a newsletter (a good one) that is well written, nicely designed, and send or deliver it monthly to every house in your community within one mile.

Let your neighbors know that your church is full of regular people. And tell the truth. For example, some were prisoners, some are former alcoholics, some are former drug addicts, some were lovers of money, some used to be full of pride, some used to be prejudiced. Let your neighbors know that the Bible says God forgives and forgets all of our sins regardless of what we've done. We can repent, and receive forgiveness, and when they're ready, you'll still be there. Accept the call to equip, educate, encourage and empower new members at all stages of their walk with Christ so they can eventually become disciples, able to help reach the lost and help them become new members. [Growth 101]

THE DIVISION

The **division** of your new members should only occur in the way they come into the church. Make sure they all attend the same class at the same time. This will help them go through class together and transition into the core membership together.

For example, new membership often happens in one of several ways:

1. Candidates for Baptism

If they're new to church and have never been baptized, show them why this is the most common option for joining the family of followers of Jesus Christ.

2. Christian Experience

If they've been a member of a church before but are now coming to your church to join, let them know this is the appropriate option.

3. Letter

Often times, members will relocate from another state and have to leave their church behind. It is your responsibility to welcome them with open arms. There may be individuals and families in this situation. For example, the fallout from Hurricane Katrina. Let them know they can come to you with a letter from their old church in such situations, if one if available.

I cannot stress how important it is for every church in this day and time to place the focus of your growth on your new members. I would add placing the focus on your youth to that statement, but that should be obvious. Without new members, and without youth in your church, your church will eventually cease to operate.

The opportunity for you to do something great for your church is sitting right before you. Use this information for what it was intended to do...help build up, edify and grow the Body of Christ. Again, it is up to you, and only you, to either 'do' or 'delegate' and whichever you do, make sure it gets 'done'.

THE DYNAMICS

The **dynamics** of what you are about to undertake if you do not already have an effective New Members Ministry, can only be described as a matter of the life and death of your church. Here's why:

Dynamic 1:   New members and youth are the lifeblood of your church. Without either and both of these groups, your church will eventually cease to operate.

Dynamic 2:   New members bring other members. Don't ever lock yourself into the mindset that new members come by themselves. If you nurture them correctly, your new member can be a source for at least five other members. How?
1) Spouse joins - other spouse will eventually follow.
2) Spouses join - 1-2 kids will most like be with them.
3) Neighbors join - same scenario...spouses and kids.

Dynamic 3:   Four times a year, your church should devote a Sunday to a new members recruitment rally. You don't have to title it that way but you should think of it that way and get your church to think about it that way.

What is a New Member Recruitment Rally? It's where you ask "each one" of the people in your church to "bring one" person to church that Sunday. If this is done, promoted, marketed and carried out correctly, you should see the size of your membership grow from inviting new members exponentially, to possibly even double.

The dynamics are endless. The result is eternal. And you should treat it that way. I'll say it again, because maybe you skipped a page or two, trying to get to the Template, but New Members are vitally important to your success & growth.

THE DESTRUCTION

The **destruction** of strongholds that the devil has over people's lives will be evident once you are well into the operation of your New Member's Ministry.

If you're a pastor reading this book, you already know this. So, the statement is not for you. It's for your new members. You should place that statement on the 2nd page of the New Member's Packet, after placing the question of "Why A New Member's Packet?"

Let your new members know that the strongholds that have been in place over their lives, now that they are a member of your church, are about to be no more. Let them know that you are equipped with the power of the Holy Spirit and the anointing that comes along with that power, to call out the demons just as Jesus did, by identifying them by name, and commanding them to leave.

Let your new members know that 'without' Jesus in their lives, there is no hope. Teach them that Jesus is the way, the truth and the life.

Teach them that anything they are dealing with in their lives, such as lying, cheating, stealing, addictions such as drug abuse, pornography, fornication, anger, and a host of other issues, are nothing more than strongholds that the devil has over their lives and that by coming to your church, they've taken the first step to surrendering to God, and giving Him the authority to begin changing them inside out.

Years from now, when you look back at the growth of your church, just remember that God placed this little small book titled *Welcome To Our Church - Guide To Creating New Member Packets* in your path when you needed it. As He always does, he knows what we need when we need it. He's an on-time God, and He's never failed us yet.

May God continue to bless your church and your ministry. Amen.

In my book: "Bearing *Fruit In A Dying World*" I discuss the tree on the cover. The tree represents your church, and each apple on the tree contains the name of someone you lead to Christ. The book asks every Christian the tough question of how much fruit you're bearing.

SUGGESTION: I would take the graphic of a tree, blow it up to life size, and use the tree to show everyone how much progress the New Member's Ministry is making. Every time a new member joins, make a public showing of letting 'them' place their apple on the tree. It will give them a sense of belonging, knowing their name is in on the church rolls, and in the Book of Life. After all, that's partly why they joined in the first place.

And, this can be a HUGE tool for motivating members who may need their fire relit.

Bearing fruit is the goal of why I wrote this book:
Welcome To Our Church, Guide to Creating New Member's Packets.
...because every Christian should tune in to the vitally important message that Jesus teaches in John 15:16 and then again, through Apostle Paul in Romans 7:4-5.

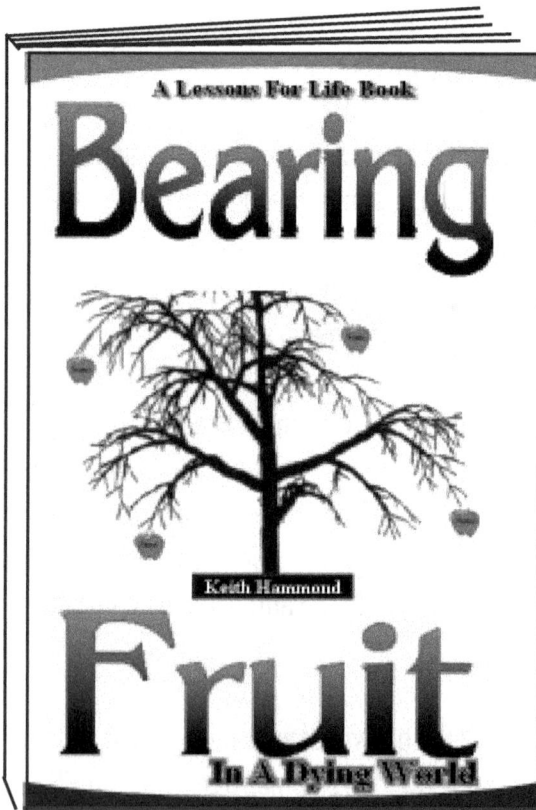

For me, the message changed my whole approach to ministry.

Section Three
The Template

NEW MEMBER PACKET
TEMPLATE
Front Cover
8.5 x 11 landscape
Download the Pagemaker & PDF file to use as a template at:
www.LessonsForLifeBooks.com/templates/NewMembers.zip

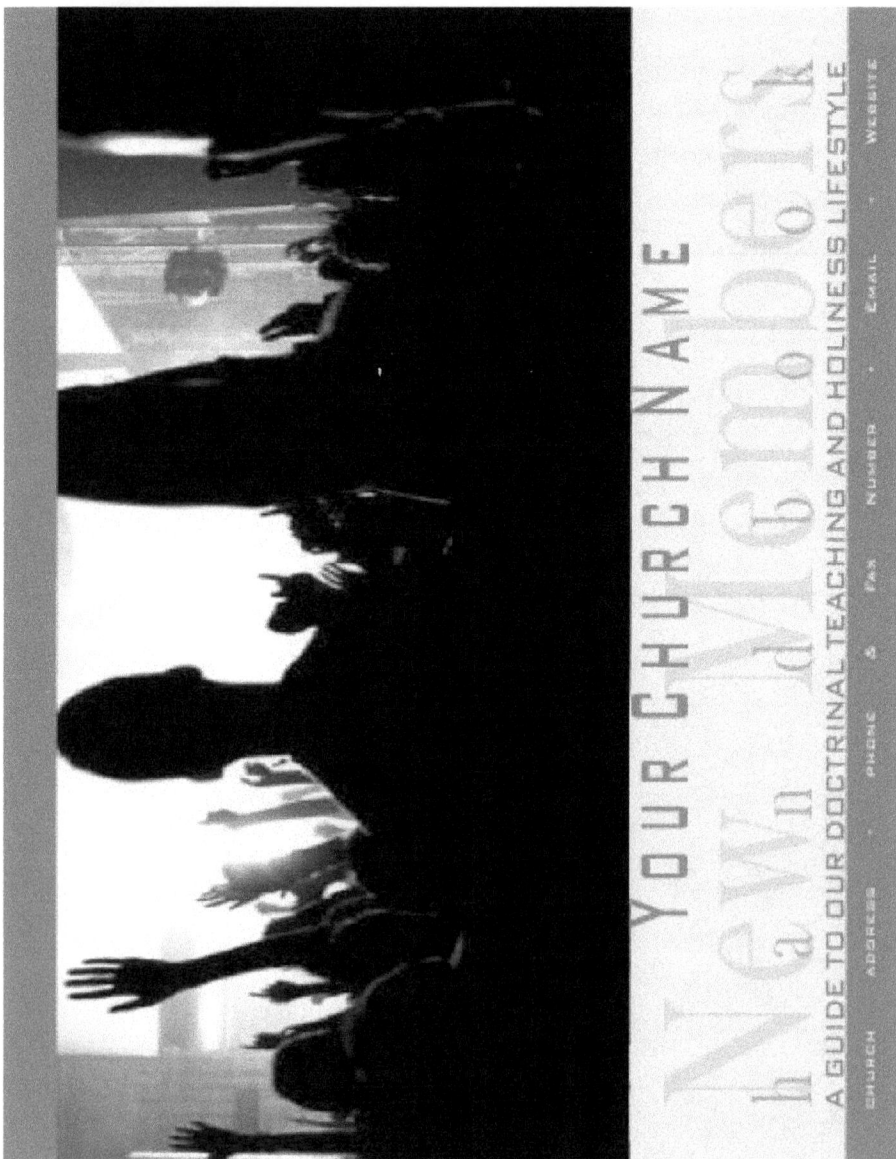

NEW MEMBER PACKET
TEMPLATE
The Pastor
8.5 x 11 landscape
Download the Pagemaker & PDF file to use as a template at:
www.LessonsForLifeBooks.com/templates/NewMembers.zip

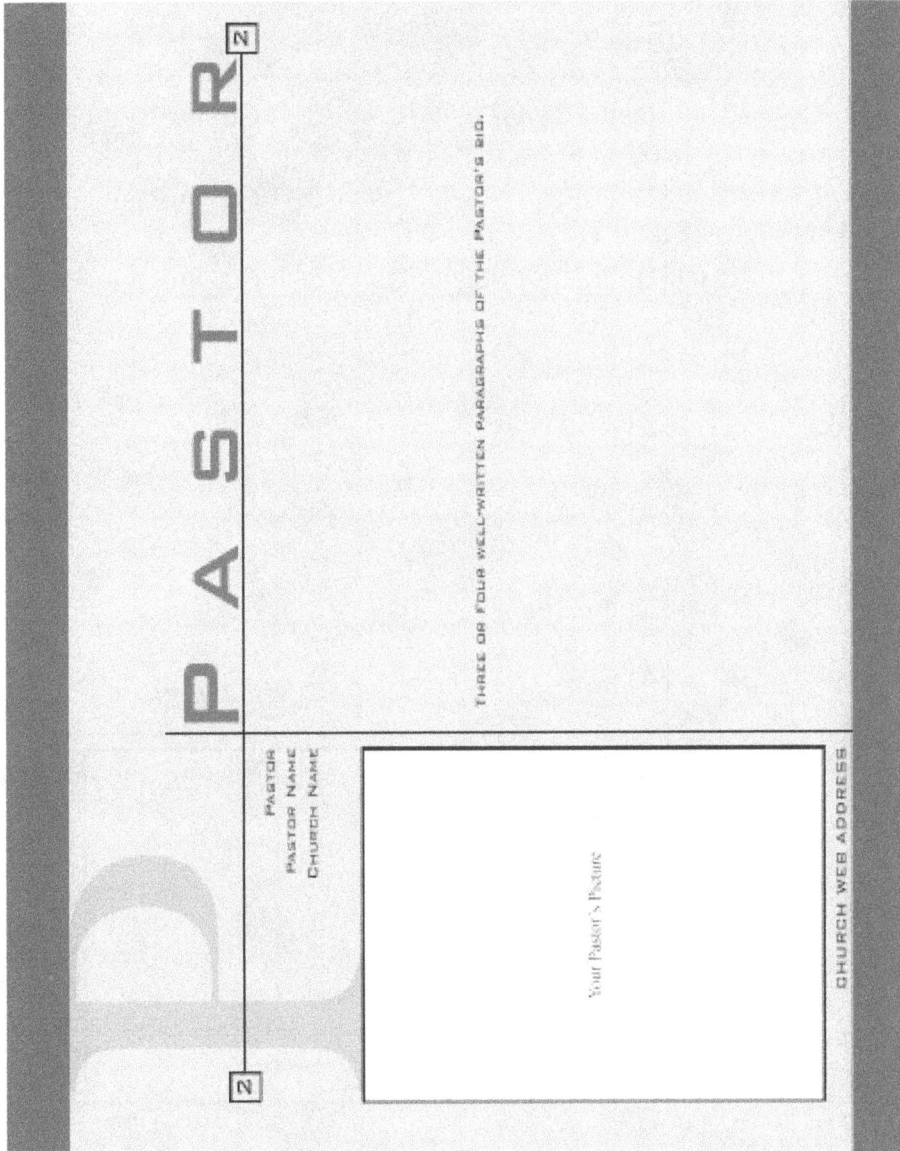

NEW MEMBER PACKET
TEMPLATE
The First Lady
8.5 x 11 landscape
Download the Pagemaker & PDF file to use as a template at:
www.LessonsForLifeBooks.com/templates/NewMembers.zip

NEW MEMBER PACKET
TEMPLATE
The Pastoral Staff
8.5 x 11 landscape
Download the Pagemaker & PDF file to use as a template at:
www.LessonsForLifeBooks.com/templates/NewMembers.zip

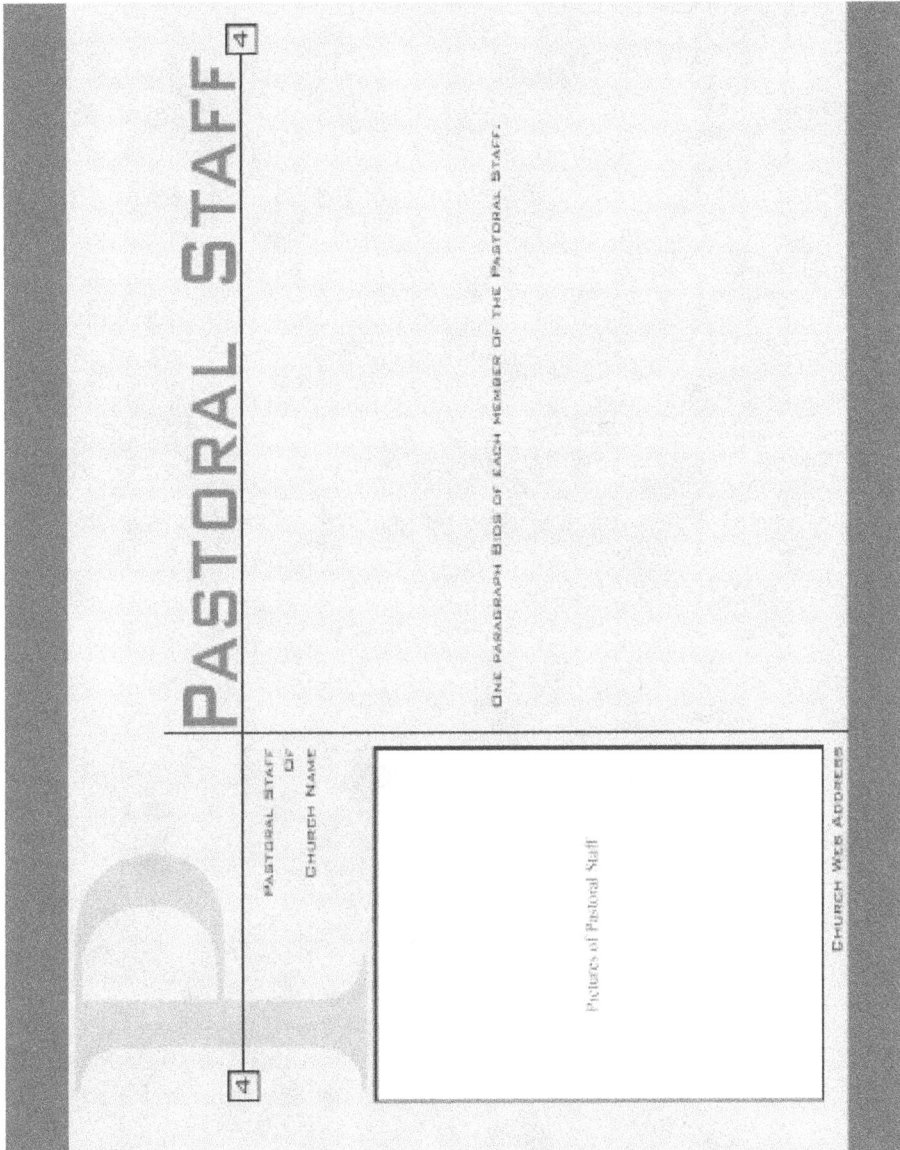

NEW MEMBER PACKET
TEMPLATE
Membership
8.5 x 11 landscape
Download the Pagemaker & PDF file to use as a template at:
www.LessonsForLifeBooks.com/templates/NewMembers.zip

MEMBERSHIP

THE MOST IMPORTANT DECISION OF YOUR LIFE

ALTHOUGH IT'S THE SLOGAN OF A WORLDLY COMPANY TODAY GOD SPOKE IT IN MALACHI 3 "MEMBERSHIP HAS ITS PRIVILEGES"

JOINING A CHURCH DOESN'T JUST MEAN THAT YOU NOW HAVE SOME PLACE TO SAY YOU GO EVERY SUNDAY. OR, THAT YOU NOW HAVE A GROUP OF PEOPLE THAT YOU CAN WORSHIP WITH, LEARN WITH, LAUGH WITH, CRY WITH, ATTEND FUNCTIONS WITH, RAISE YOUR KIDS WITH, AND TRUST, ETC. YOU CAN GET THESE THINGS JUST ABOUT ANYWHERE.

JOINING A CHURCH MEANS SOMETHING MORE IMPORTANT THAN ALL OF THESE THINGS COMBINED. THE PRIMARY REASON YOU JOIN A CHURCH IS TO KNOW THAT YOU ARE NOW A PART OF GOD'S FAMILY. AND THAT IS THE FIRST STEP TO HAVING ACCESS TO GOD, OTHER MEMBERS OF HIS FAMILY, EVERY ONE OF HIS PROMISES, HIS PROTECTION, AND HIS RESOURCES.

THE COMMITMENT TAKES SURRENDER, SACRIFICE, REPENTANCE, AND A HOST OF THINGS THAT YOU WILL BEGIN TO DISCOVER AND LEARN ABOUT.

BECOMING A PART OF GOD'S FAMILY AND THE COMMITMENT TO JOIN A CHURCH MEANS EVERYTHING IN YOUR LIFE. IT IS THE MOST IMPORTANT DECISION YOU WILL EVER MAKE. IT IS BOTH LIFE-CHANGING AND LIFE-ALTERING, AND HERE'S A LITTLE INFORMATION ON WHY.

WHEN YOU JOIN A CHURCH:

• PEOPLE STILL LOST IN THE WORLD WILL NO LONGER TREAT YOU THE SAME
• YOU WILL HAVE TO SACRIFICE BEING AROUND CERTAIN PEOPLE
• YOUR FLESH WILL FIGHT AGAINST EVERY DECISION YOU MAKE FOR GOD.

THESE THINGS ARE NORMAL FOR NEW CHRISTIANS. BUT STAY IN CHURCH AND STAY COMMITTED TO COMING REGULARLY SO YOU CAN GET STRONGER.

CHURCH WEB ADDRESS

NEW MEMBER PACKET
TEMPLATE
Contents
8.5 x 11 landscape
Download the Pagemaker & PDF file to use as a template at:
www.LessonsForLifeBooks.com/templates/NewMembers.zip

CONTENTS

THE CONTENTS OF THIS
NEW MEMBER'S HANDBOOK
IS DESIGNED TO GIVE YOU
AN OVERVIEW OF OUR CHURCH.

IT IS A BASIC GUIDE TO OUR DOCTRINAL
TEACHINGS
AND HOLINESS LIFESTYLE

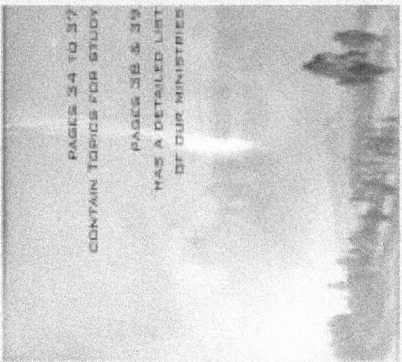

PAGES 34 TO 37
CONTAIN TOPICS FOR STUDY

PAGES 38 & 39
HAS A DETAILED LIST
OF OUR MINISTRIES

CHURCH WEB ADDRESS

NEW MEMBER PACKET
TEMPLATE
Welcome
8.5 x 11 landscape

Download the Pagemaker & PDF file to use as a template at:
www.LessonsForLifeBooks.com/templates/NewMembers.zip

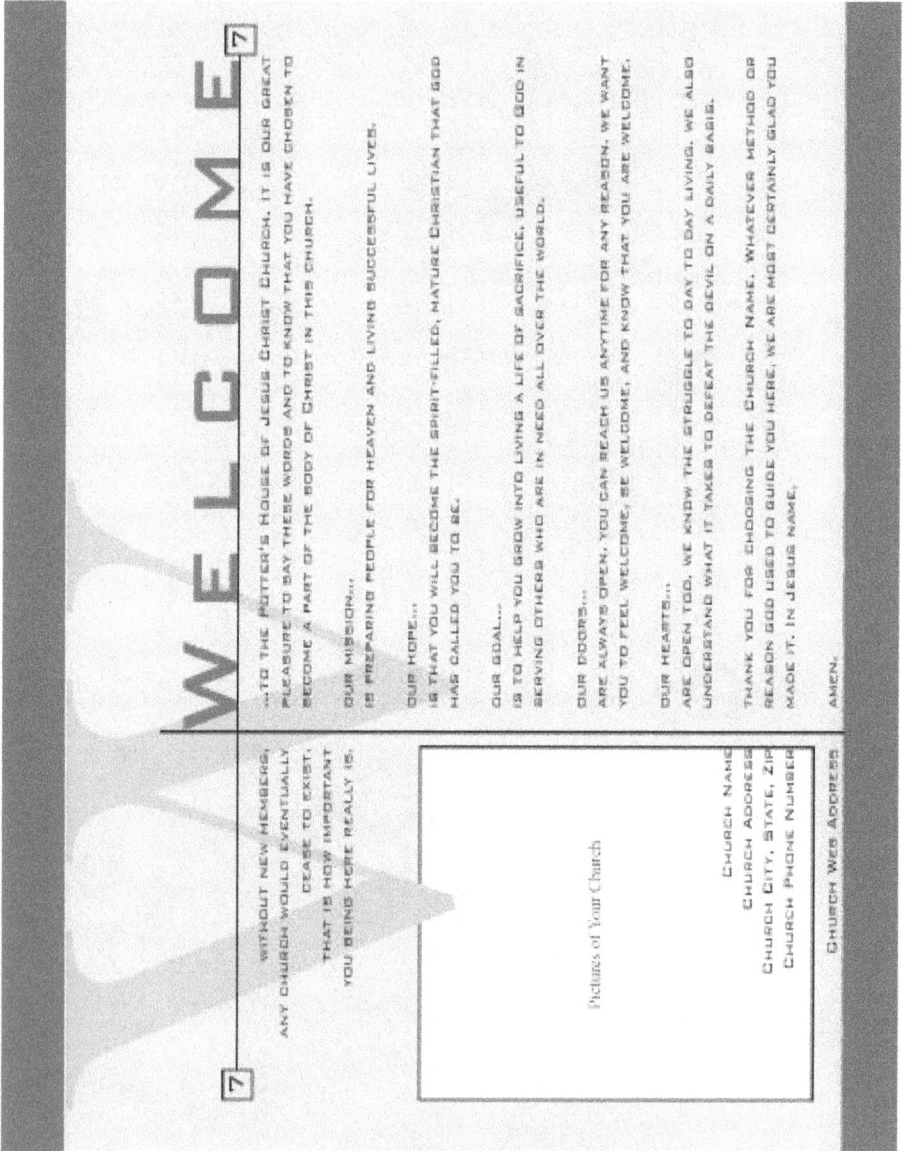

WELCOME

...TO THE POTTER'S HOUSE OF JESUS CHRIST CHURCH. IT IS OUR GREAT PLEASURE TO SAY THESE WORDS AND TO KNOW THAT YOU HAVE CHOSEN TO BECOME A PART OF THE BODY OF CHRIST IN THIS CHURCH.

OUR MISSION...
IS PREPARING PEOPLE FOR HEAVEN AND LIVING SUCCESSFUL LIVES.

OUR HOPE...
IS THAT YOU WILL BECOME THE SPIRIT-FILLED, MATURE CHRISTIAN THAT GOD HAS CALLED YOU TO BE.

OUR GOAL...
IS TO HELP YOU GROW INTO LIVING A LIFE OF SACRIFICE, USEFUL TO GOD IN SERVING OTHERS WHO ARE IN NEED ALL OVER THE WORLD.

OUR DOORS...
ARE ALWAYS OPEN. YOU CAN REACH US ANYTIME FOR ANY REASON. WE WANT YOU TO FEEL WELCOME, BE WELCOME, AND KNOW THAT YOU ARE WELCOME.

OUR HEARTS...
ARE OPEN TOO. WE KNOW THE STRUGGLE TO DAY TO DAY LIVING. WE ALSO UNDERSTAND WHAT IT TAKES TO DEFEAT THE DEVIL ON A DAILY BASIS.

THANK YOU FOR CHOOSING THE CHURCH NAME. WHATEVER METHOD OR REASON GOD USED TO GUIDE YOU HERE, WE ARE MOST CERTAINLY GLAD YOU MADE IT. IN JESUS NAME,

AMEN.

WITHOUT NEW MEMBERS, ANY CHURCH WOULD EVENTUALLY CEASE TO EXIST. THAT IS HOW IMPORTANT YOU BEING HERE REALLY IS.

Picture of Your Church

CHURCH NAME
CHURCH ADDRESS
CHURCH CITY, STATE, ZIP
CHURCH PHONE NUMBER

CHURCH WEB ADDRESS

NEW MEMBER PACKET TEMPLATE
Introduction
8.5 x 11 landscape
Download the Pagemaker & PDF file to use as a template at:
www.LessonsForLifeBooks.com/templates/NewMembers.zip

I N T R O

IF YOU'VE BEEN THINKING, PRAYING, SEARCHING, AND HOPING FOR A PLACE TO GET ESTABLISHED IN GOD'S WORD AND HIS WILL YOU'VE FOUND IT

THE CHURCH NAME IS A NON-DENOMINATIONAL CHURCH THAT STRICTLY TEACHES, PREACHES, AND WHOLE-HEARTEDLY BELIEVES IN THE HOLY (SCRIPTURES) BIBLE. WE BELIEVE EVERYONE TODAY MUST BE BORN-AGAIN OF THE WATER AND OF THE SPIRIT, MEANING: WATER BAPTIZED IN JESUS NAME AND HAVE THE HOLY (SPIRIT) GHOST WITH SPEAKING IN OTHER TONGUES AS THE SPIRIT GIVES UTTERANCE. WE BELIEVE IN ACTS 2:38 FOR SALVATION.

THE CHURCH NAME WELCOMES EVERYONE REGARDLESS OF RACE OR NATIONALITY TO COME TO ANY AND ALL OF OUR SERVICES. WE ARE NOT CONCERNED ABOUT HOW AN INDIVIDUAL IS DRESSED, JUST COME AS YOU ARE. WE BELIEVE IN LIVING A HOLY AND SANCTIFIED LIFESTYLE JUST AS THE BIBLE ADMONISH US TO IN I PETER 1:16- "BECAUSE IT IS WRITTEN, BE YE HOLY; FOR I AM HOLY."

THE CHURCH NAME IS A CHURCH THAT BELIEVES IN EACH INDIVIDUAL FREELY PRAISING AND WORSHIPING GOD AS YOU FEEL LEAD BY THE HOLY SPIRIT. WHETHER IT IS RUNNING, JUMPING, CRYING, SINGING, CLAPPING, SHOUTING, AND DANCING IN THE SPIRIT, WE ARE AN EMOTIONAL AND ENERGETIC CHURCH.

AT THE CHURCH NAME, WE DO NOT TEACH AGAINST WOMEN WEARING PANTS, MAKE-UP, OR JEWELRY TO CHURCH. JUST THINK MODEST AND LET THE HOLY SPIRIT LEAD YOU. THESE ARE JUST A FEW INSIGHTS ABOUT THE CHURCH NAME AND WHAT THIS HANDBOOK IS ALL ABOUT. WE HOPE THIS INTRODUCTION WETS YOUR APPETITE ENOUGH SO THAT YOU ARE EAGER AND EXCITED ABOUT READING THIS NEW MEMBERS HANDBOOK. WELCOME TO THE CHURCH NAME!!!!!!!!

Picture of Your Congregation

CHURCH WEB ADDRESS

NEW MEMBER PACKET
TEMPLATE
Tithing
8.5 x 11 landscape
Download the Pagemaker & PDF file to use as a template at:
www.LessonsForLifeBooks.com/templates/NewMembers.zip

TITHING

TITHING IS AN ESSENTIAL PART OF WORSHIP.

TITHING IS REQUIRED OF EVERY MEMBER OF EVERY CHURCH. IT IS NOT JUST SOMETHING THAT IS ONLY DONE AT CHURCH NAME.

GOD REQUIRES IT OF US. HE ASKS FOR 10% OF THE FIRSTFRUITS OF ALL OUR INCREASE. DETAILS ARE IN MALACHI CHAPTER 3:6-12, BUT THERE ARE MANY, MANY OTHER REFERENCES TO TITHING ALL THROUGHOUT THE BIBLE. HERE ARE A FEW:

GENESIS 14:20
"AND HE GAVE HIM TITHES OF ALL."

II CORINTHIANS 9:6
"BUT THIS I SAY, HE WHICH SOWETH SPARINGLY SHALL REAP ALSO SPAR-INGLY; AND HE WHICH SOWETH BOUNTIFULLY SHALL ALSO REAP BOUNTI-FULLY"

II CORINTHIANS 9:7
EVERY MAN ACCORDING AS HE PURPOSETH IN HIS HEART, SO LET HIM GIVE; NOT GRUDGINGLY OR OF NECESSITY, FOR GOD LOVES A CHEERFUL GIVER"

AS SAINTS OF GOD, WE KNOW AND ARE KEENLY AWARE THAT MOST PEOPLE SPEND THEIR TIME WORKING, THINKING, HOPING, STRIVING FOR WHATEVER IT IS THAT THEY ARE PASSIONATE ABOUT. WE ARE ALSO KNOWLEGEABLE ABOUT THE FACT THAT THE VERY THING MOST PEOPLE SPEND MOST OF THEIR TIME ON, IS WHERE OR WHAT THEY SPEND MOST OF THEIR MONEY ON.

AT CHURCH NAME, TITHING IS A WAY OF LIFE. GOD GETS BACK THE FIRST OF EVERYTHING HE GIVES TO US.

CHURCH WEB ADDRESS

NEW MEMBER PACKET
TEMPLATE
History
8.5 x 11 landscape
Download the Pagemaker & PDF file to use as a template at:
www.LessonsForLifeBooks.com/templates/NewMembers.zip

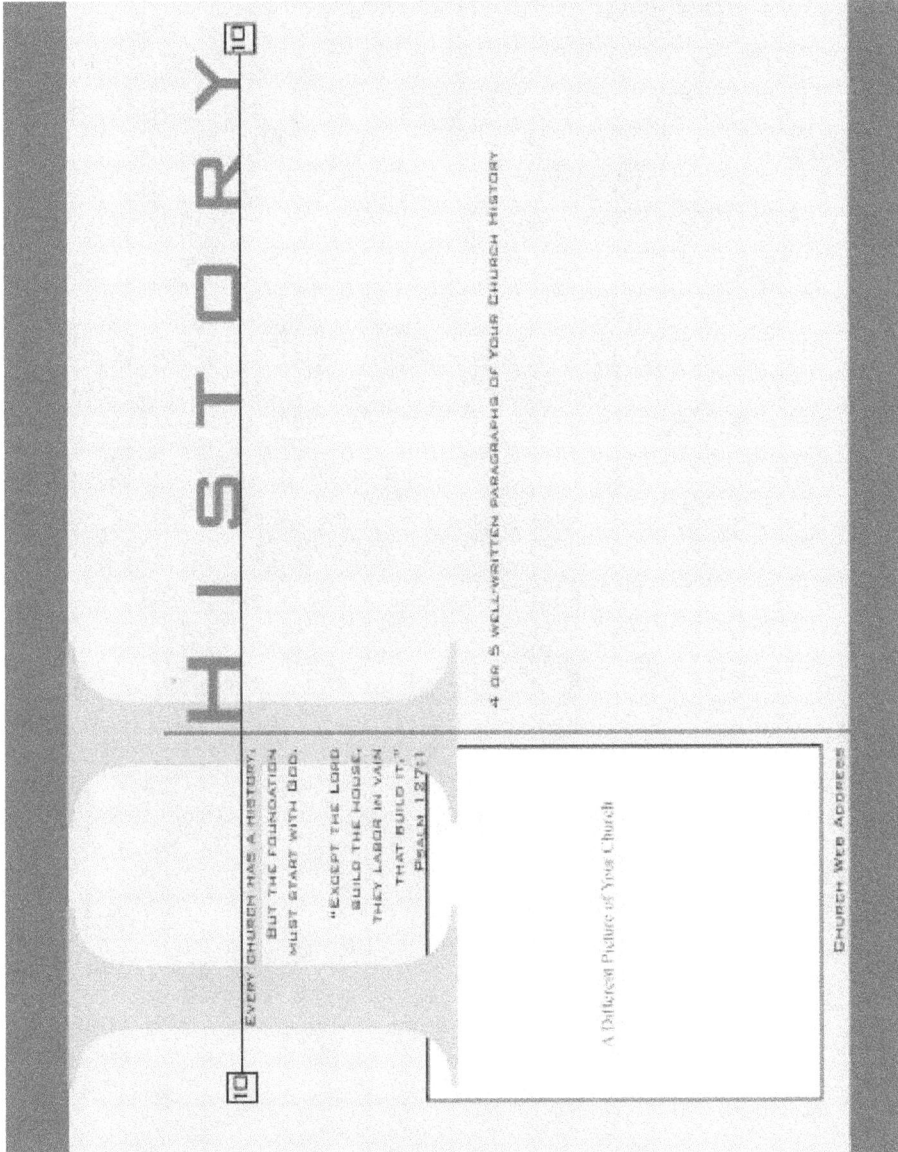

HISTORY

EVERY CHURCH HAS A HISTORY, BUT THE FOUNDATION MUST START WITH GOD.

"EXCEPT THE LORD BUILD THE HOUSE, THEY LABOR IN VAIN THAT BUILD IT."
PSALM 127:1

4 OR 5 WELL-WRITTEN PARAGRAPHS OF YOUR CHURCH HISTORY

A Different Picture of Your Church

CHURCH WEB ADDRESS

NEW MEMBER PACKET
TEMPLATE
Growth
8.5 x 11 landscape
Download the Pagemaker & PDF file to use as a template at:
www.LessonsForLifeBooks.com/templates/NewMembers.zip

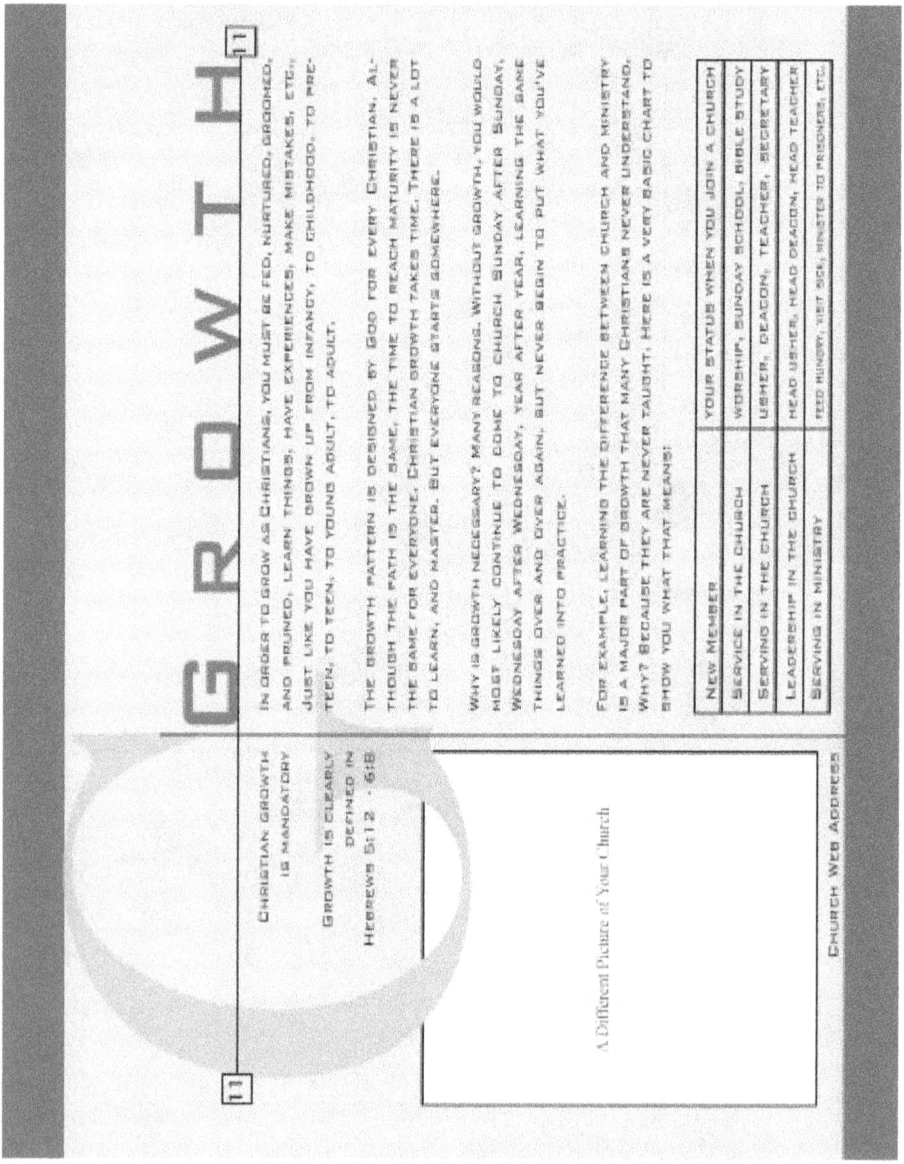

The template content (rotated) reads:

G R O W T H

IN ORDER TO GROW AS CHRISTIANS, YOU MUST BE FED, NURTURED, GROOMED, AND PRUNED. LEARN THINGS, HAVE EXPERIENCES, MAKE MISTAKES, ETC., JUST LIKE YOU HAVE GROWN UP FROM INFANCY, TO CHILDHOOD, TO PRE-TEEN, TO TEEN, TO YOUNG ADULT, TO ADULT.

THE GROWTH PATTERN IS DESIGNED BY GOD FOR EVERY CHRISTIAN. AL-THOUGH THE PATH IS THE SAME, THE TIME TO REACH MATURITY IS NEVER THE SAME FOR EVERYONE. CHRISTIAN GROWTH TAKES TIME. THERE IS A LOT TO LEARN, AND MASTER. BUT EVERYONE STARTS SOMEWHERE.

WHY IS GROWTH NECESSARY? MANY REASONS. WITHOUT GROWTH, YOU WOULD MOST LIKELY CONTINUE TO COME TO CHURCH SUNDAY AFTER SUNDAY, WEDNESDAY AFTER WEDNESDAY, YEAR AFTER YEAR, LEARNING THE SAME THINGS OVER AND OVER AGAIN. BUT NEVER BEGIN TO PUT WHAT YOU'VE LEARNED INTO PRACTICE.

FOR EXAMPLE, LEARNING THE DIFFERENCE BETWEEN CHURCH AND MINISTRY IS A MAJOR PART OF GROWTH THAT MANY CHRISTIANS NEVER UNDERSTAND. WHY? BECAUSE THEY ARE NEVER TAUGHT. HERE IS A VERY BASIC CHART TO SHOW YOU WHAT THAT MEANS:

	YOUR STATUS WHEN YOU JOIN A CHURCH
NEW MEMBER	WORSHIP, SUNDAY SCHOOL, BIBLE STUDY
SERVICE IN THE CHURCH	USHER, DEACON, TEACHER, SECRETARY
SERVING IN THE CHURCH	HEAD USHER, HEAD DEACON, HEAD TEACHER
LEADERSHIP IN THE CHURCH	FEED HUNGRY, VISIT SICK, MINISTER TO PRISONERS, ETC.
SERVING IN MINISTRY	

CHRISTIAN GROWTH IS MANDATORY

GROWTH IS CLEARLY DEFINED IN Hebrews 5:12 - 6:8

A Different Picture of Your Church

CHURCH WEB ADDRESS

NEW MEMBER PACKET
TEMPLATE
Our Beliefs
8.5 x 11 landscape
Download the Pagemaker & PDF file to use as a template at:
www.LessonsForLifeBooks.com/templates/NewMembers.zip

OUR BELIEFS

[12]

At Church Name we believe in God, Jesus Christ as Son of God, and the Holy Spirit. Here are the SEVEN BIBLICAL PRINCIPLES that we hold to:

1. WE BELIEVE
The Bible is the infallible Word of God written by Holy Men as the Holy Ghost inspired them to write; II Peter 1:20.

2. WE BELIEVE
You must repent and be baptized in water by immersion in the name of our Lord and Savior Jesus Christ for the remission (removal) of sins; and the baptism of the Holy Ghost, speaking in other tongues as the Spirit gives the utterance. This is the "new birth experience"; Acts 1:8 and Acts 2:38.

3. WE BELIEVE
Jesus Christ is God in the flesh. We believe in the virgin birth; that Jesus was born both human and divine. God manifested in the flesh; Matthew 1:21; 1st Timothy 3:16.

4. WE BELIEVE
In the death, burial, and resurrection of Jesus Christ. We believe that He ascended on high and sent His Spirit, the Holy Ghost, which was poured out at Jerusalem over 2000 years ago and we believe that it is still filling the hearts of believers on today; Luke 24:46-49, Acts chapter 2.

5. WE BELIEVE
In a holy, sanctified life. Divine healing, laying on hands, working of miracles in Jesus name and we believe in the glorious catching away (rapture) of the saints when Jesus returns in the clouds of glory to take His people to Heaven; Luke 10:19; 1st Thess. 4:16-17.

6. WE BELIEVE
That in Jesus Christ dwelleth all the fullness of the Godhead bodily, Col. 2:9.

7. WE BELIEVE
In remembering the sufferings of Jesus Christ through Holy Communion through drinking of the blood (non alcoholic) and eating of the body (bread) of Jesus. I Cor. 11:23-26.

Thou shalt have no other Gods before me

Thou shalt not make unto thee any graven image

The name of the Lord thy God in vain

Remember the Sabbath day

Honour thy father and thy mother

Thou shalt not kill

Thou shalt not commit adultery

Thou shalt not steal

Thou shalt not bear false witness against thy neighbor

Thou shalt not covet

Church Web Address

[12]

NEW MEMBER PACKET
TEMPLATE

Do Your Part

8.5 x 11 landscape

Download the Pagemaker & PDF file to use as a template at:
www.LessonsForLifeBooks.com/templates/NewMembers.zip

DO YOUR PART

"FOR AS THE BODY IS ONE, AND HATH MANY MEMBERS, AND ALL THE MEMBERS OF THAT ONE BODY, BEING MANY, ARE ONE BODY: SO ALSO IS CHRIST."

1ST CORINTHIANS 12:12

THIS IS THE MOST CLEARLY DEFINED SCRIPTURE ON PARTS OF THE BODY OF CHRIST. IF YOU READ FURTHER, YOU LEARN THAT JUST LIKE OUR BODIES HAVE HEADS, NECKS, SHOULDERS, ARMS, HANDS, ETC., ALL THE WAY DOWN TO OUR FEET, THE CHURCH IS NO DIFFERENT. HOW? BECAUSE JESUS CHRIST IS THE HEAD OF THE CHURCH, AND WE, AS MEMBERS OF THE CHURCH, ARE PART OF HIS BODY.

THAT'S WHY DOING YOUR PART IS SO IMPORTANT. YOU HAVE BEEN GIFTED WITH SPECIAL SKILLS THAT POSSIBLY NO ONE ELSE HAS EXCEPT YOU. NO ONE CAN PREACH LIKE YOUR PASTOR, AND HE CAN'T DO WHATEVER IT IS THAT YOU DO. AND EACH OF YOUR PARTS IS EQUALLY IMPORTANT.

THE BIBLE EXPLAINS IT LIKE THIS: "IF THE FOOT SHALL SAY, BECAUSE I AM NOT THE EYE, I AM NOT OF THE BODY; IT IS THEREFORE NOT OF THE BODY?"

HERE'S ANOTHER EXAMPLE. YOUR PASTOR IS RESPONSIBLE FOR PREACHING AND TEACHING THE GOSPEL OF JESUS CHRIST TO EVERYONE IN THE CHURCH. LET'S SAY YOU'RE RESPONSIBLE FOR CREATING MATERIALS SUCH AS FLYERS, BANNERS, BOOKLETS, HANDBOOKS, POSTERS, TRACTS, AND OTHER THINGS THAT HELP SPREAD THE GOSPEL OF JESUS CHRIST TO EVERYONE IN AND OUTSIDE THE CHURCH. BOTH ASSIGNMENTS ARE EQUALLY IMPORTANT.

WHATEVER YOUR ASSIGNMENT, WHATEVER YOU ARE GIFTED AT, DO YOUR BEST TO DO YOUR PART TO HELP SUPPORT THE CHURCH AND THE MINISTRY.

PREACHING • TEACHING
ADMINISTRATING • GOVERNING
SINGING • USHERING
GREETING • ORGANIZING
DRAWING • WRITING
EDITING • PROGRAMMING
FUNDRAISING • FEEDING
REACHING • COMFORTING

EVERY PART OF THE BODY IS ESSENTIAL

CHURCH WEB ADDRESS

NEW MEMBER PACKET
TEMPLATE
Acts 2:38
8.5 x 11 landscape
Download the Pagemaker & PDF file to use as a template at:
www.LessonsForLifeBooks.com/templates/NewMembers.zip

Acts 2:38

14

"THEN PETER SAID UNTO THEM, REPENT, AND BE BAPTIZED EVERY ONE OF YOU IN THE NAME OF JESUS CHRIST FOR THE REMISSION OF SINS, AND YE SHALL RECEIVE THE GIFT OF THE HOLY GHOST."

IN FACT, IF YOU READ FURTHER INTO THE NEXT SEVERAL CHAPTERS OF THE BOOK OF ACTS, YOU'LL LEARN THAT UNLESS CERTAIN THINGS ARE DONE IN THE NAME OF JESUS, THEY JUST WON'T WORK. GOOD INTENTIONS, BUT NO POWER BEHIND THE ACTIONS.

FLESH AND BLOOD CAN'T GET INTO THE KINGDOM OF HEAVEN. AND UNLESS YOU ARE BORN OF WATER AND OF THE SPIRIT, YOU CANNOT ENTER INTO THE KINGDOM OF GOD (JOHN 3:5).

THERE ARE MANY THINGS THAT ORDINARY CHRISTIANS DO IN THE CHURCH AND IN MINISTRY, BUT BY FAR, THIS IS THE MOST IMPORTANT.

AND, THERE ARE MANY THINGS THAT ORDINARY CHRISTIANS DO IN THE CHURCH AND THE MINISTRY, BELIEVING THEY ARE SAVED. BUT GOD'S WORD IS VERY CLEAR ABOUT THE PROCESS. AND UNLESS YOU HAVE THE HOLY SPIRIT THERE IS NO CHANCE OF GETTING INTO HEAVEN WHEN JESUS RETURNS.

THE BIBLE SAYS THAT WHEN JESUS RETURNS EVERYONE WHO HAS THE HOLY SPIRIT WILL RECEIVE A GLORIFIED BODY. THAT MEANS THE BODY WE CURRENTLY HAVE WILL BE CHANGED IN THE BLINK OF AN EYE INTO SOMETHING THAT CAN ONLY EXIST IN, LIVE IN, AND BE MANIFEST IN HEAVEN.

I DON'T KNOW ABOUT YOU, BUT I AM TRULY LOOKING FORWARD TO NO LONGER WORRYING ABOUT SICKNESS AND HEALTH ONCE JESUS RETURNS!

THE ONLY SCRIPTURE THAT PROVIDES THE FULL PROCESS OF BEING SAVED.

CHURCH WEB ADDRESS

14

NEW MEMBER PACKET
TEMPLATE
Leadership
8.5 x 11 landscape
Download the Pagemaker & PDF file to use as a template at:
www.LessonsForLifeBooks.com/templates/NewMembers.zip

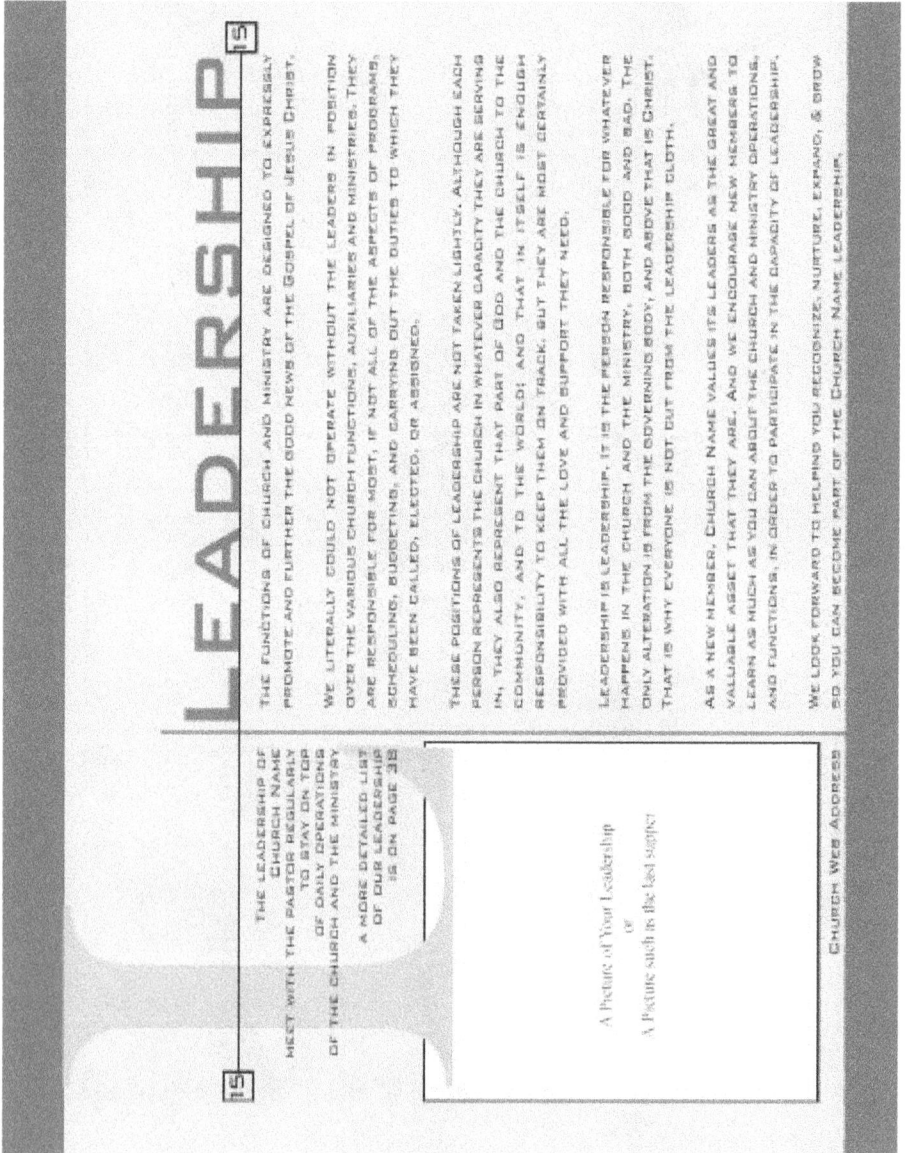

LEADERSHIP

THE LEADERSHIP OF CHURCH NAME MEET WITH THE PASTOR REGULARLY TO STAY ON TOP OF DAILY OPERATIONS OF THE CHURCH AND THE MINISTRY

A MORE DETAILED LIST OF OUR LEADERSHIP IS ON PAGE 28

THE FUNCTIONS OF CHURCH AND MINISTRY ARE DESIGNED TO EXPRESSLY PROMOTE AND FURTHER THE GOOD NEWS OF THE GOSPEL OF JESUS CHRIST.

WE LITERALLY COULD NOT OPERATE WITHOUT THE LEADERS IN POSITION OVER THE VARIOUS CHURCH FUNCTIONS, AUXILIARIES AND MINISTRIES. THEY ARE RESPONSIBLE FOR MOST, IF NOT ALL OF THE ASPECTS OF PROGRAMS, SCHEDULING, BUDGETING, AND CARRYING OUT THE DUTIES TO WHICH THEY HAVE BEEN CALLED, ELECTED, OR ASSIGNED.

THESE POSITIONS OF LEADERSHIP ARE NOT TAKEN LIGHTLY. ALTHOUGH EACH PERSON REPRESENTS THE CHURCH IN WHATEVER CAPACITY THEY ARE SERVING IN, THEY ALSO REPRESENT THAT PART OF GOD AND THE CHURCH TO THE COMMUNITY, AND TO THE WORLD! AND THAT IN ITSELF IS ENOUGH RESPONSIBILITY TO KEEP THEM ON TRACK, BUT THEY ARE MOST CERTAINLY PROVIDED WITH ALL THE LOVE AND SUPPORT THEY NEED.

LEADERSHIP IS LEADERSHIP. IT IS THE PERSON RESPONSIBLE FOR WHATEVER HAPPENS IN THE CHURCH AND THE MINISTRY, BOTH GOOD AND BAD. THE ONLY ALTERATION IS FROM THE GOVERNING BODY, AND ABOVE THAT IS CHRIST. THAT IS WHY EVERYONE IS NOT OUT FROM THE LEADERSHIP CLOTH.

AS A NEW MEMBER, CHURCH NAME VALUES ITS LEADERS AS THE GREAT AND VALUABLE ASSET THAT THEY ARE. AND WE ENCOURAGE NEW MEMBERS TO LEARN AS MUCH AS YOU CAN ABOUT THE CHURCH AND MINISTRY OPERATIONS, AND FUNCTIONS, IN ORDER TO PARTICIPATE IN THE CAPACITY OF LEADERSHIP.

WE LOOK FORWARD TO HELPING YOU RECOGNIZE, NURTURE, EXPAND, & GROW SO YOU CAN BECOME PART OF THE CHURCH NAME LEADERSHIP.

A Picture of Your Leadership
or
A Picture such as the last image

CHURCH WEB ADDRESS

NEW MEMBER PACKET
TEMPLATE
List Of Ministries
8.5 x 11 landscape
Download the Pagemaker & PDF file to use as a template at:
www.LessonsForLifeBooks.com/templates/NewMembers.zip

LIST OF MINISTRIES

ONE OF THE FIRST QUESTIONS MANY NEW MEMBERS ASK IS, "WHERE DO I FIT IN?" OR, "HOW CAN I GET INVOLVED?" THIS BRIEF LIST OF MINISTRIES IS THE FIRST STEP TOWARD SEEING WHERE YOUR GIFTS CAN BE MOST USEFUL. UNDERSTAND THIS, YOUR GIFTS, WHATEVER THEY MAY BE, ARE MOST LIKELY ALWAYS NEEDED SOME PART OF THE CHURCH OR THE MINISTRY. FOR A MORE COMPREHENSIVE LIST, PLEASE CONTACT THE CHURCH ADMINISTRATOR.

#1 ORGANIZATION YOU SUPPORT
MINISTRY LOCATION, CITY, PHONE AND HOW YOU SUPPORT THEM.

#2 ORGANIZATION YOU SUPPORT
MINISTRY LOCATION, CITY, PHONE AND HOW YOU SUPPORT THEM.

#3 ORGANIZATION YOU SUPPORT
MINISTRY LOCATION, CITY, PHONE AND HOW YOU SUPPORT THEM.

#4 ORGANIZATION YOU SUPPORT
MINISTRY LOCATION, CITY, PHONE AND HOW YOU SUPPORT THEM.

#5 ORGANIZATION YOU SUPPORT
MINISTRY LOCATION, CITY, PHONE AND HOW YOU SUPPORT THEM.

#6 ORGANIZATION YOU SUPPORT
MINISTRY LOCATION, CITY, PHONE AND HOW YOU SUPPORT THEM.

#7 ORGANIZATION YOU SUPPORT
MINISTRY LOCATION, CITY, PHONE AND HOW YOU SUPPORT THEM.

#8 ORGANIZATION YOU SUPPORT
MINISTRY LOCATION, CITY, PHONE AND HOW YOU SUPPORT THEM.

CHURCH NAME IS COMMITTED TO CREATING MINISTRIES THAT MEET THE NEEDS OF OUR MEMBERS AND PEOPLE IN NEED LOCALLY AND INTERNATIONALLY

AND,

WE REGULARLY SUPPORT THE CAUSES LISTED BELOW

A MORE DETAILED LIST OF OUR MINISTRIES AND THEIR LEADERSHIP IS ON PAGES 38 & 39

A Picture of The Logos
of the organizations
Your Church Regularly Supports
through volunteerism or donation

CHURCH WEB ADDRESS

69

NEW MEMBER PACKET
TEMPLATE

The Members
8.5 x 11 landscape
Download the Pagemaker & PDF file to use as a template at:
www.LessonsForLifeBooks.com/templates/NewMembers.zip

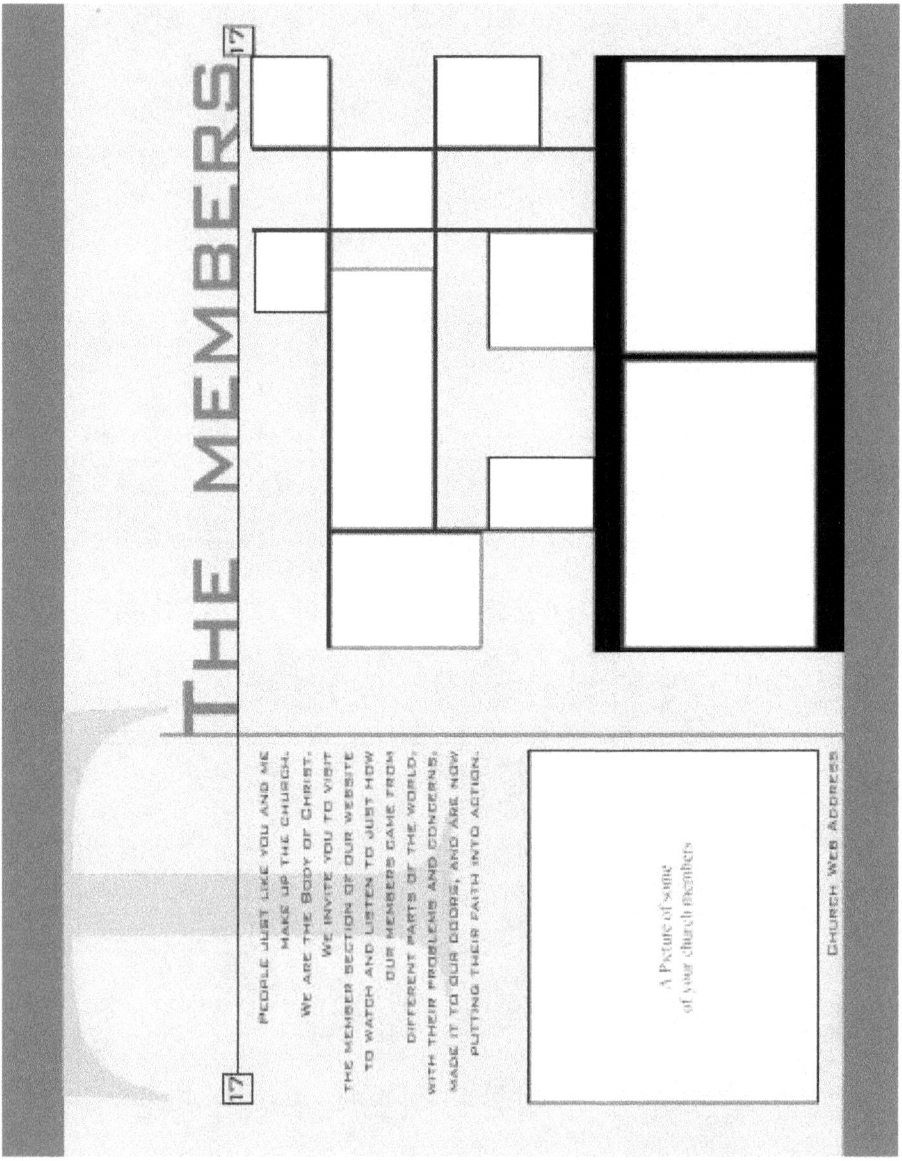
17
THE MEMBERS
17
PEOPLE JUST LIKE YOU AND ME
MAKE UP THE CHURCH.
WE ARE THE BODY OF CHRIST.
WE INVITE YOU TO VISIT
THE MEMBER SECTION OF OUR WEBSITE
TO WATCH AND LISTEN TO JUST HOW
OUR MEMBERS CAME FROM
DIFFERENT PARTS OF THE WORLD,
WITH THEIR PROBLEMS AND CONCERNS,
MADE IT TO OUR DOORS, AND ARE NOW
PUTTING THEIR FAITH INTO ACTION.
A Picture of some
of your church members
CHURCH WEB ADDRESS

NEW MEMBER PACKET
TEMPLATE
Holy Spirit
8.5 x 11 landscape
Download the Pagemaker & PDF file to use as a template at:
www.LessonsForLifeBooks.com/templates/NewMembers.zip

NEW MEMBER PACKET
TEMPLATE
Individuality
8.5 x 11 landscape
Download the Pagemaker & PDF file to use as a template at:
www.LessonsForLifeBooks.com/templates/NewMembers.zip

INDIVIDUALITY

AS PART OF THE BODY OF CHRIST YOU ARE STILL AN INDIVIDUAL BUT CONSIDERED A VITAL PART OF THE ENTIRE BODY

INDIVIDUAL PARTS MAKE UP THE WHOLE OF THE BODY OF JESUS CHRIST. EACH PART, WHETHER IT BE THE EYES, HANDS, OR FEET, ARE AS VITAL AS THE OTHERS.

THINK ABOUT IT, THE HANDS CAN'T DO THE JOB OF THE FEET, THE EYES CAN'T DO THE JOB OF THE MOUTH, AND SO ON. EACH PART HAS A PURPOSE.

MAINTAINING YOUR INDIVIDUALITY AS A MEMBER OF THE BODY OF CHRIST, IS JUST AS IMPORTANT AS BEING A PART OF THE WHOLE BODY. WHY? BECAUSE THERE ARE GIFTS THAT YOU HAVE BEEN GIVEN BY THE HOLY SPIRIT THAT WERE NOT GIVEN TO ANYONE ELSE. AND YOU ARE CALLED BY GOD TO BRING THAT GIFT INTO THE CHURCH TO BE A PART OF A LARGER PURPOSE.

IMAGINE A CHURCH WHERE EVERYONE HAD THE EXACT SAME GIFTS. AND THAT GIFT IS AS A SECRETARY. WHO WOULD PREACH? WHO WOULD TEACH? WHO WOULD GREET AND SEAT PEOPLE? WHO WOULD OVERSEE THE OPERATIONS OF THE CHURCH? WHO WOULD CLEAN THE CHURCH? WHO WOULD PLAY THE MUSIC? WHO WOULD SING?

SO YOU CAN SEE, ONE INDIVIDUAL PERSON CANNOT DO ALL THE JOBS AND FUNCTIONS OF THE WHOLE CHURCH. IT TAKES MANY PEOPLE. AND, IT SOMETIMES TAKES PEOPLE WITH MULTIPLE GIFTS TO WEAR MANY HATS UNTIL SOMEONE ELSE COMES ALONG WHO CAN HELP FILL THE GAPS.

YOUR INDIVIDUALITY IS IMPORTANT TO MAINTAIN, BUT YOU MUST ALSO DESIRE TO BECOME PART OF A LARGER BODY OF OTHER CHRISTIANS FOR A MUCH LARGER PURPOSE. GOD'S PURPOSE FOR CHRISTIANS DOESN'T JUST STOP WHEN YOU GET TO YOUR CHURCH. HIS MASTER PLAN IS GLOBAL.

CHURCH WEB ADDRESS

NEW MEMBER PACKET
TEMPLATE
Newsletter
8.5 x 11 landscape
Download the Pagemaker & PDF file to use as a template at:
www.LessonsForLifeBooks.com/templates/NewMembers.zip

NEW MEMBER PACKET
TEMPLATE
Gifts
8.5 x 11 landscape
Download the Pagemaker & PDF file to use as a template at:
www.LessonsForLifeBooks.com/templates/NewMembers.zip

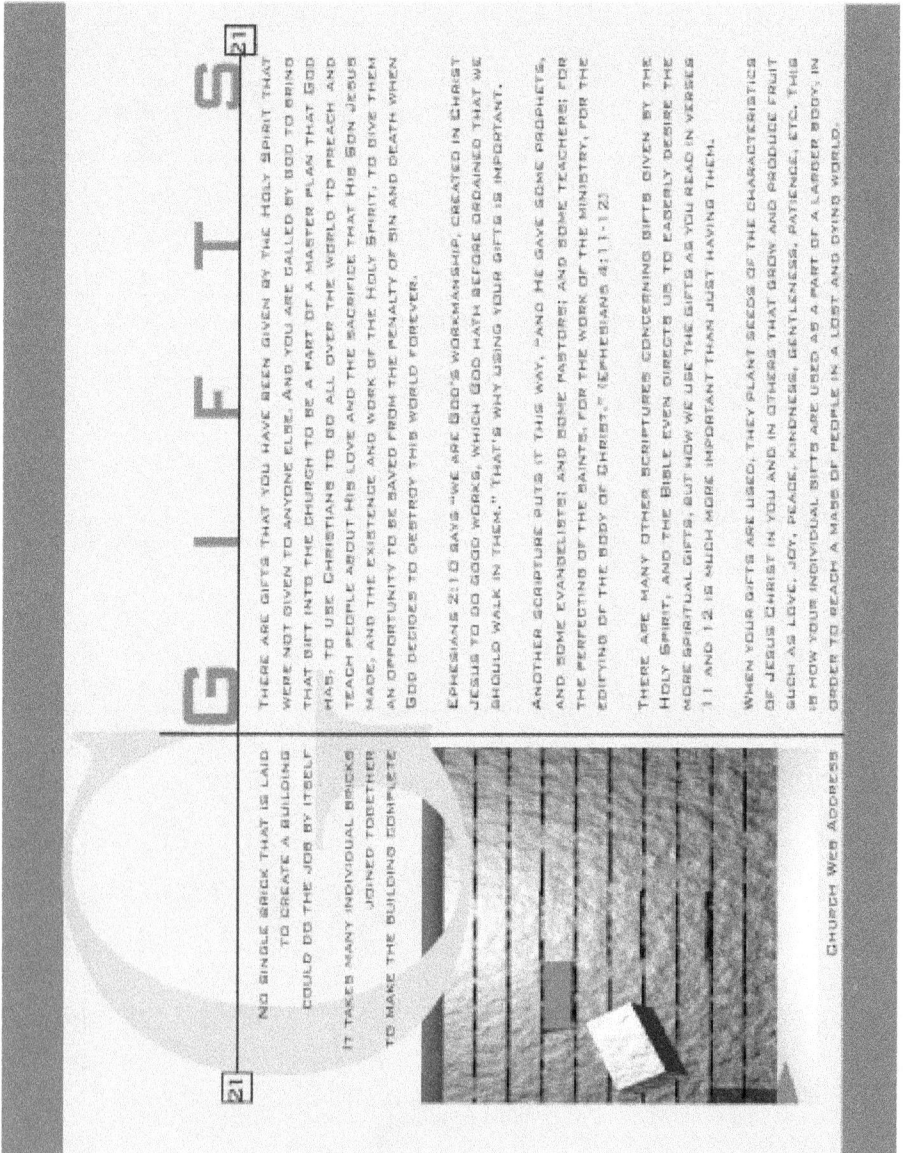

GIFTS 21

THERE ARE GIFTS THAT YOU HAVE BEEN GIVEN BY THE HOLY SPIRIT THAT WERE NOT GIVEN TO ANYONE ELSE. AND YOU ARE CALLED BY GOD TO BRING THAT GIFT INTO THE CHURCH TO BE A PART OF A MASTER PLAN THAT GOD HAS, TO USE CHRISTIANS TO GO ALL OVER THE WORLD TO PREACH AND TEACH PEOPLE ABOUT HIS LOVE AND THE SACRIFICE THAT HIS SON JESUS MADE, AND THE EXISTENCE AND WORK OF THE HOLY SPIRIT, TO GIVE THEM AN OPPORTUNITY TO BE SAVED FROM THE PENALTY OF SIN AND DEATH WHEN GOD DECIDES TO DESTROY THIS WORLD FOREVER.

EPHESIANS 2:10 SAYS "WE ARE GOD'S WORKMANSHIP, CREATED IN CHRIST JESUS TO DO GOOD WORKS, WHICH GOD HATH BEFORE ORDAINED THAT WE SHOULD WALK IN THEM." THAT'S WHY USING YOUR GIFTS IS IMPORTANT.

ANOTHER SCRIPTURE PUTS IT THIS WAY, "AND HE GAVE SOME PROPHETS, AND SOME EVANGELISTS; AND SOME PASTORS; AND SOME TEACHERS; FOR THE PERFECTING OF THE SAINTS, FOR THE WORK OF THE MINISTRY, FOR THE EDIFYING OF THE BODY OF CHRIST." (EPHESIANS 4:11-12)

THERE ARE MANY OTHER SCRIPTURES CONCERNING GIFTS GIVEN BY THE HOLY SPIRIT, AND THE BIBLE EVEN DIRECTS US TO EAGERLY DESIRE THE MORE SPIRITUAL GIFTS. BUT HOW WE USE THE GIFTS AS YOU READ IN VERSES 11 AND 12 IS MUCH MORE IMPORTANT THAN JUST HAVING THEM.

WHEN YOUR GIFTS ARE USED, THEY PLANT SEEDS OF THE CHARACTERISTICS OF JESUS CHRIST IN YOU AND IN OTHERS THAT GROW AND PRODUCE FRUIT SUCH AS LOVE, JOY, PEACE, KINDNESS, GENTLENESS, PATIENCE, ETC. THIS IS HOW YOUR INDIVIDUAL GIFTS ARE USED AS A PART OF A LARGER BODY, IN ORDER TO REACH A MASS OF PEOPLE IN A LOST AND DYING WORLD.

NO SINGLE BRICK THAT IS LAID TO CREATE A BUILDING COULD DO THE JOB BY ITSELF

IT TAKES MANY INDIVIDUAL BRICKS JOINED TOGETHER TO MAKE THE BUILDING COMPLETE

CHURCH WEB ADDRESS

21

NEW MEMBER PACKET
TEMPLATE
Sacrifice
8.5 x 11 landscape
Download the Pagemaker & PDF file to use as a template at:
www.LessonsForLifeBooks.com/templates/NewMembers.zip

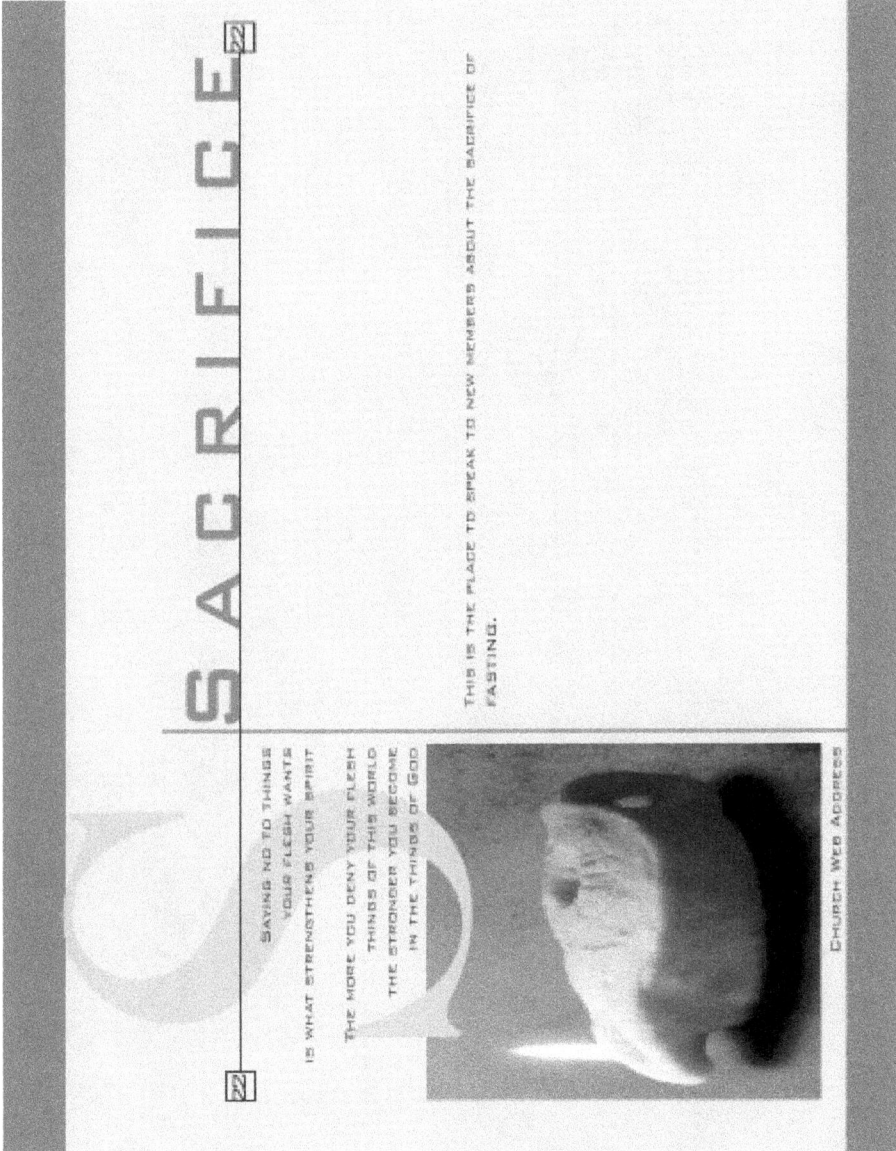

NEW MEMBER PACKET
TEMPLATE
Answers
8.5 x 11 landscape
Download the Pagemaker & PDF file to use as a template at:
www.LessonsForLifeBooks.com/templates/NewMembers.zip

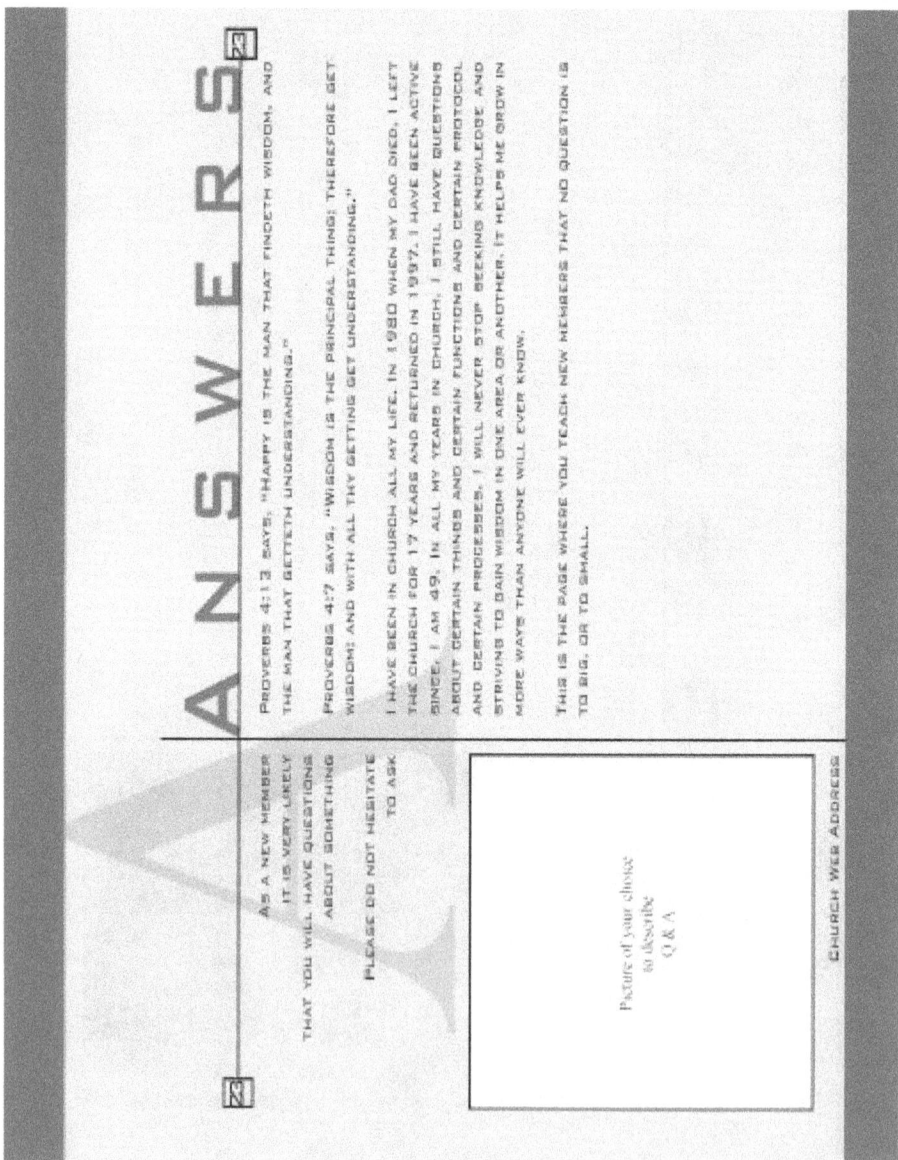

ANSWERS ®

PROVERBS 4:13 SAYS, "HAPPY IS THE MAN THAT FINDETH WISDOM, AND THE MAN THAT GETTETH UNDERSTANDING."

PROVERBS 4:7 SAYS, "WISDOM IS THE PRINCIPAL THING; THEREFORE GET WISDOM: AND WITH ALL THY GETTING GET UNDERSTANDING."

I HAVE BEEN IN CHURCH ALL MY LIFE. IN 1980 WHEN MY DAD DIED, I LEFT THE CHURCH FOR 17 YEARS AND RETURNED IN 1997. I HAVE BEEN ACTIVE SINCE. I AM 49. IN ALL MY YEARS IN CHURCH, I STILL HAVE QUESTIONS ABOUT CERTAIN THINGS AND CERTAIN FUNCTIONS AND CERTAIN PROTOCOL AND CERTAIN PROCESSES. I WILL NEVER STOP SEEKING KNOWLEDGE AND STRIVING TO GAIN WISDOM IN ONE AREA OR ANOTHER. IT HELPS ME GROW IN MORE WAYS THAN ANYONE WILL EVER KNOW.

THIS IS THE PAGE WHERE YOU TEACH NEW MEMBERS THAT NO QUESTION IS TO BIG, OR TO SMALL.

AS A NEW MEMBER IT IS VERY LIKELY THAT YOU WILL HAVE QUESTIONS ABOUT SOMETHING

PLEASE DO NOT HESITATE TO ASK

Picture of your choice
to describe
Q & A

CHURCH WEB ADDRESS

NEW MEMBER PACKET
TEMPLATE
Relationships
8.5 x 11 landscape
Download the Pagemaker & PDF file to use as a template at:
www.LessonsForLifeBooks.com/templates/NewMembers.zip

NEW MEMBER PACKET
TEMPLATE
Education
8.5 x 11 landscape
Download the Pagemaker & PDF file to use as a template at:
www.LessonsForLifeBooks.com/templates/NewMembers.zip

NEW MEMBER PACKET
TEMPLATE
Prayer
8.5 x 11 landscape
Download the Pagemaker & PDF file to use as a template at:
www.LessonsForLifeBooks.com/templates/NewMembers.zip

PRAYER

MEMBERS OF CHURCH NAME HAVE FORMED RELATIONSHIPS WITH EACH OTHER THROUGH PRAYER.

AS PRAYER PARTNERS, TWO MEMBERS, OR A GROUP OF MEMBERS, COME TOGETHER IN PERSON, OR ON THE PHONE, TO PRAY ABOUT MANY THINGS.

IF YOU LISTEN TO THE TESTIMONY OF THE MEMBERS, YOU WILL SEE THAT THIS PROCESS HAS HELPED MANY OF THEM GROW BY LEAPS AND BOUNDS OVER WHAT THEY WERE USED TO TRADITIONALLY AT OTHER CHURCHES.

PRAYER CHANGES THINGS. GOD HEARS THE CRY OF THOSE HE'S CONNECTED TO. IT IS HOW WE COMMUNICATE WITH GOD AND HOW WE CAST OUR CARES UPON HIM BECAUSE HE CARES FOR US. THE PRAYERS OF A RIGHTEOUS MAN AVAILETH MUCH. THAT MEANS THEY GET THROUGH. THEY HAVE IMPACT. THEY REACH GOD IN A WAY THAT OTHERS CANNOT.

AS A NEW MEMBER, GIVE YOURSELF CONTINUALLY TO PRAYER AND WATCH IT BEGIN TO CHANGE THINGS IN YOUR LIFE.

ASK SOMEONE, CONNECT WITH SOMEONE, FIND A PRAYER PARTNER OR A PRAYER GROUP AND WATCH WHAT HAPPENS.

BE COMMITTED TO PRAYER. STAY COMMITTED TO PRAYER. STAY PRAYED UP. IT HELPS STRENGTHEN YOUR DEFENSES AGAINST ANYTHING THE DEVIL TRIES TO THROW AT YOU. YOU WILL FIND THAT PRAYER IS A VALUABLE TOOL IN THE WALK AS A NEW MEMBER AND IT CAN AND WILL HELP YOU THROUGH MANY SITUATIONS. SO GET IN YOUR PRAYER CLOSET AND START TALKING TO GOD. DON'T WORRY ABOUT NOT KNOWING HOW TO PRAY, WE WILL HELP YOU LEARN.

MANY MEMBERS OF CHURCH NAME HAVE BEEN PRAYING TOGETHER OVER THE PHONE LATE AT NIGHT OR EARLY IN THE MORNING FOR MANY YEARS

PRAYER REQUEST LINE CHURCH PHONE NUMBER

Picture of person praying hands

CHURCH WEB ADDRESS

NEW MEMBER PACKET
TEMPLATE
Outreach
8.5 x 11 landscape
Download the Pagemaker & PDF file to use as a template at:
www.LessonsForLifeBooks.com/templates/NewMembers.zip

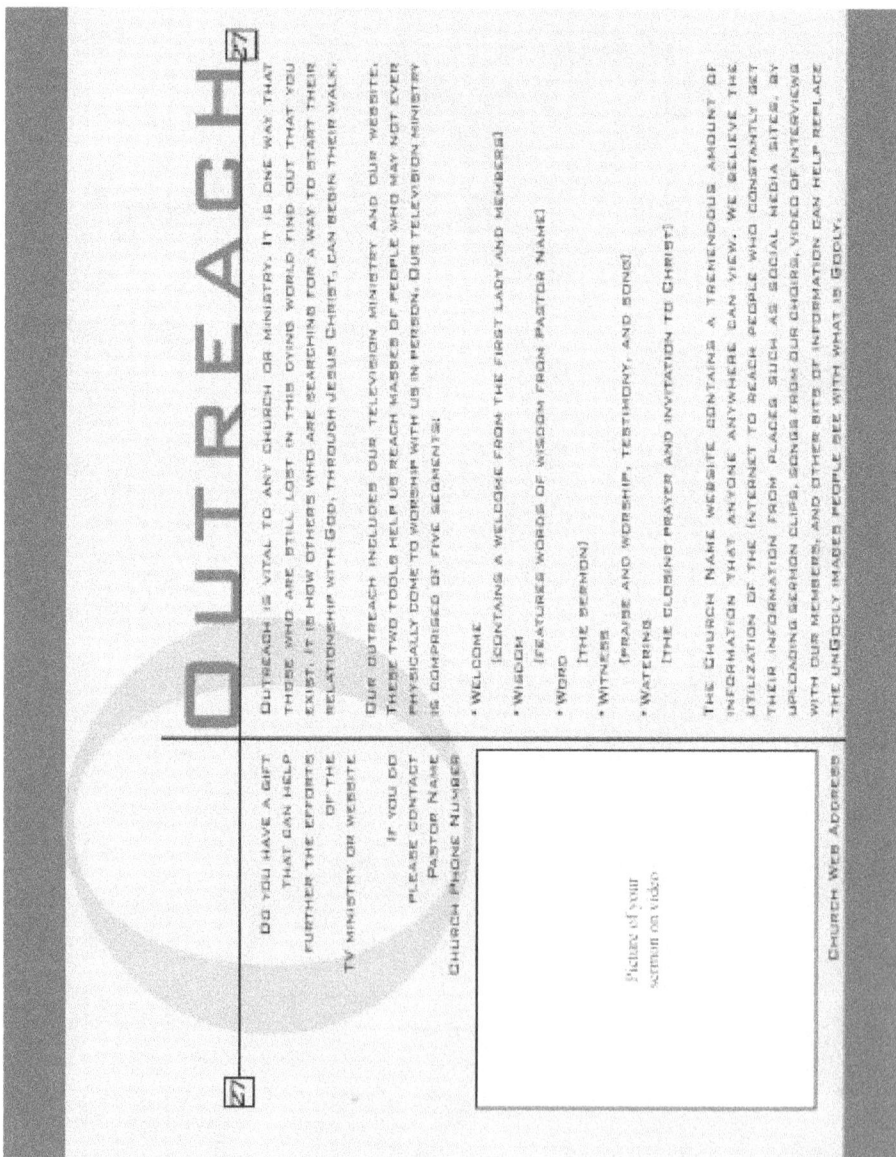

NEW MEMBER PACKET
TEMPLATE
Services
8.5 x 11 landscape
Download the Pagemaker & PDF file to use as a template at:
www.LessonsForLifeBooks.com/templates/NewMembers.zip

SERVICES

CHURCH NAME SERVICES ARE DETAILED IN THE CALENDAR ON OUR WEBSITE, AND IN THE WEEKLY BULLETIN AT CHURCH ON SUNDAY.

HERE IS A BRIEF LIST OF OUR WORSHIP AND EDUCATION SERVICES:

SUNDAY
FAMILY WORSHIP SERVICE .... TIME

WEDNESDAY
FAMILY BIBLE SCHOOL .... TIME

FRIDAY
FAMILY WORSHIP SERVICE .... TIME

COMMUNION
IS NORMALLY DONE X TIMES PER YEAR

PROBABLY THE MOST IMPORTANT PAGE OF THIS HANDBOOK IS THIS ONE

WHY?

BECAUSE IT TELLS YOU WHEN WE COME TOGETHER AND WORSHIP GOD

Picture of your worship service

CHURCH WEB ADDRESS

NEW MEMBER PACKET
TEMPLATE
Schedule
8.5 x 11 landscape
Download the Pagemaker & PDF file to use as a template at:
www.LessonsForLifeBooks.com/templates/NewMembers.zip

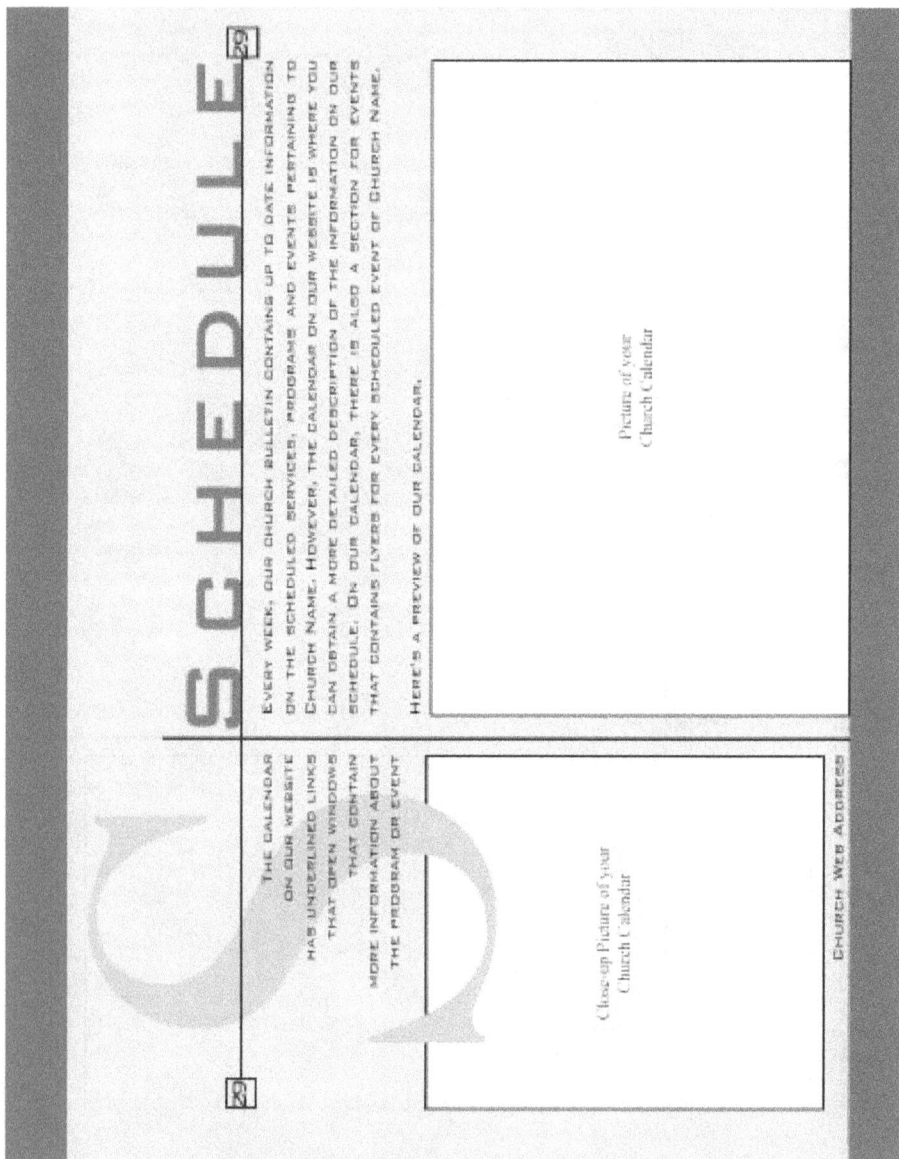

NEW MEMBER PACKET
TEMPLATE
Input
8.5 x 11 landscape
Download the Pagemaker & PDF file to use as a template at:
www.LessonsForLifeBooks.com/templates/NewMembers.zip

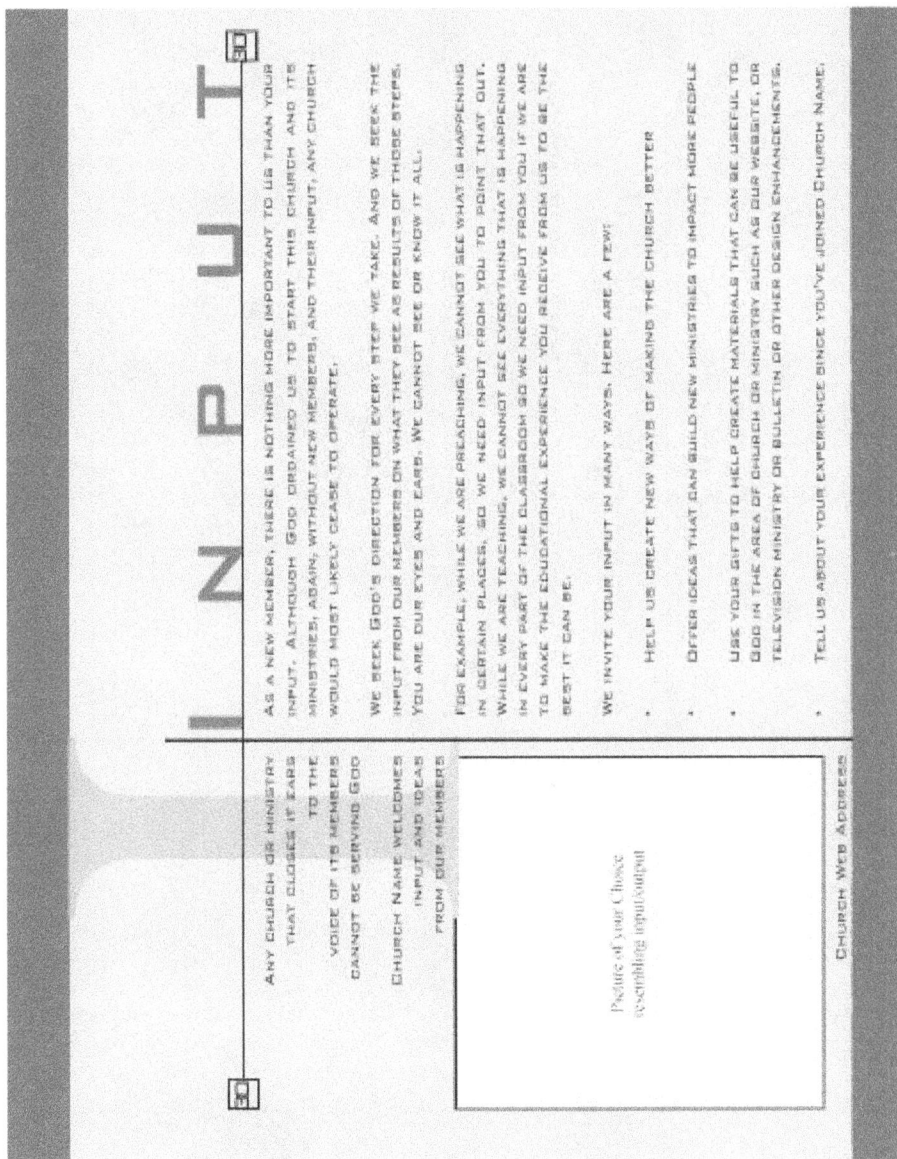

INPUT

AS A NEW MEMBER, THERE IS NOTHING MORE IMPORTANT TO US THAN YOUR INPUT. ALTHOUGH GOD ORDAINED US TO START THIS CHURCH AND ITS MINISTRIES, AGAIN, WITHOUT NEW MEMBERS, AND THEIR INPUT, ANY CHURCH WOULD MOST LIKELY CEASE TO OPERATE.

WE SEEK GOD'S DIRECTION FOR EVERY STEP WE TAKE, AND WE SEEK THE INPUT FROM OUR MEMBERS ON WHAT THEY SEE AS RESULTS OF THOSE STEPS. YOU ARE OUR EYES AND EARS. WE CANNOT SEE OR KNOW IT ALL.

FOR EXAMPLE, WHILE WE ARE PREACHING, WE CANNOT SEE WHAT IS HAPPENING IN CERTAIN PLACES. SO WE NEED INPUT FROM YOU TO POINT THAT OUT. WHILE WE ARE TEACHING, WE CANNOT SEE EVERYTHING THAT IS HAPPENING IN EVERY PART OF THE CLASSROOM SO WE NEED INPUT FROM YOU IF WE ARE TO MAKE THE EDUCATIONAL EXPERIENCE YOU RECEIVE FROM US TO BE THE BEST IT CAN BE.

WE INVITE YOUR INPUT IN MANY WAYS. HERE ARE A FEW!

- HELP US CREATE NEW WAYS OF MAKING THE CHURCH BETTER

- OFFER IDEAS THAT CAN BUILD NEW MINISTRIES TO IMPACT MORE PEOPLE

- USE YOUR GIFTS TO HELP CREATE MATERIALS THAT CAN BE USEFUL TO GOD IN THE AREA OF CHURCH OR MINISTRY SUCH AS OUR WEBSITE, OR TELEVISION MINISTRY OR BULLETIN OR OTHER DESIGN ENHANCEMENTS.

- TELL US ABOUT YOUR EXPERIENCE SINCE YOU'VE JOINED CHURCH NAME,

ANY CHURCH OR MINISTRY THAT CLOSES IT EARS TO THE VOICE OF ITS MEMBERS CANNOT BE SERVING GOD

CHURCH NAME WELCOMES INPUT AND IDEAS FROM OUR MEMBERS

Picture of your Choice

CHURCH WEB ADDRESS

NEW MEMBER PACKET
TEMPLATE
Baptism
8.5 x 11 landscape
Download the Pagemaker & PDF file to use as a template at:
www.LessonsForLifeBooks.com/templates/NewMembers.zip

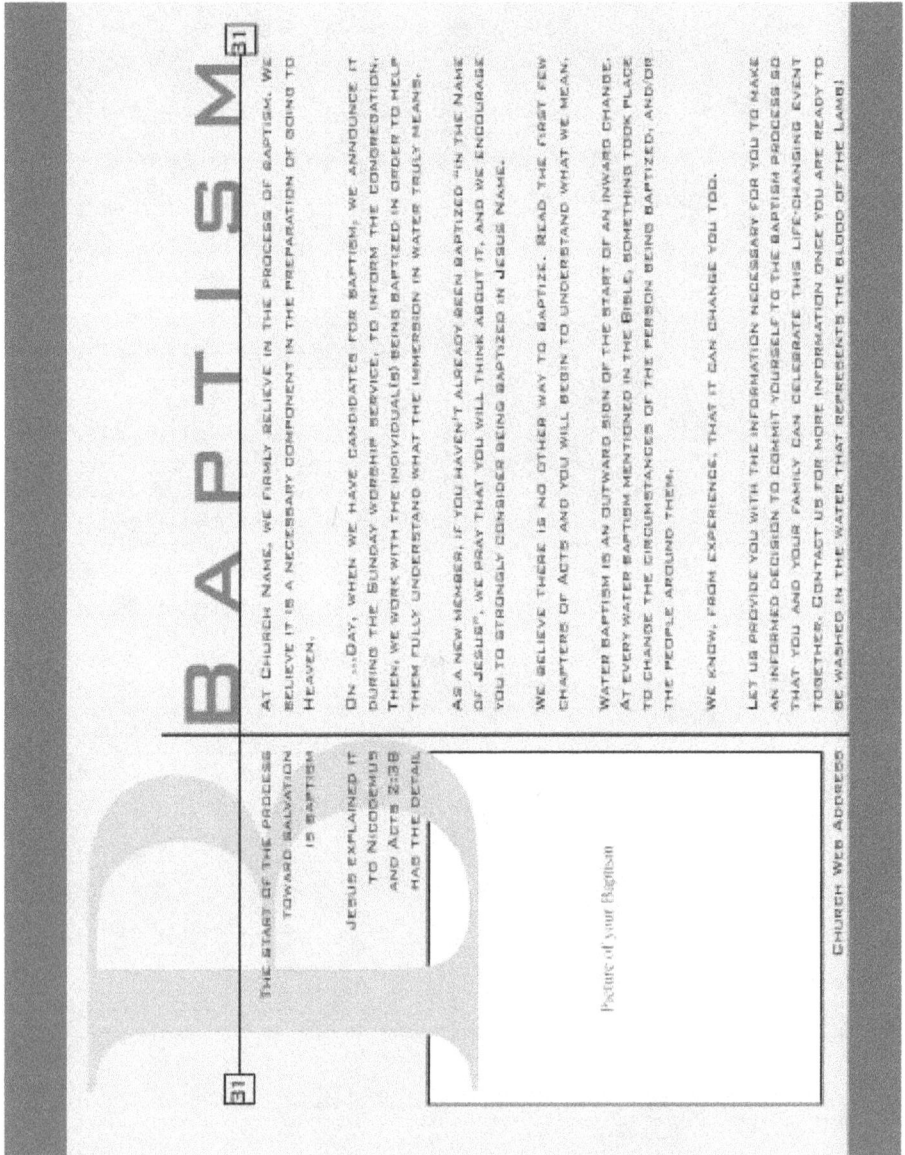

BAPTISM

AT CHURCH NAME, WE FIRMLY BELIEVE IN THE PROCESS OF BAPTISM. WE BELIEVE IT IS A NECESSARY COMPONENT IN THE PREPARATION OF GOING TO HEAVEN.

ON ...DAY, WHEN WE HAVE CANDIDATES FOR BAPTISM, WE ANNOUNCE IT DURING THE SUNDAY WORSHIP SERVICE, TO INFORM THE CONGREGATION. THEN, WE WORK WITH THE INDIVIDUAL(S) BEING BAPTIZED IN ORDER TO HELP THEM FULLY UNDERSTAND WHAT THE IMMERSION IN WATER TRULY MEANS.

AS A NEW MEMBER, IF YOU HAVEN'T ALREADY BEEN BAPTIZED "IN THE NAME OF JESUS", WE PRAY THAT YOU WILL THINK ABOUT IT, AND WE ENCOURAGE YOU TO STRONGLY CONSIDER BEING BAPTIZED IN JESUS NAME.

WE BELIEVE THERE IS NO OTHER WAY TO BAPTIZE. READ THE FIRST FEW CHAPTERS OF ACTS AND YOU WILL BEGIN TO UNDERSTAND WHAT WE MEAN.

WATER BAPTISM IS AN OUTWARD SIGN OF THE START OF AN INWARD CHANGE. AT EVERY WATER BAPTISM MENTIONED IN THE BIBLE, SOMETHING TOOK PLACE TO CHANGE THE CIRCUMSTANCES OF THE PERSON BEING BAPTIZED, AND/OR THE PEOPLE AROUND THEM.

WE KNOW, FROM EXPERIENCE, THAT IT CAN CHANGE YOU TOO.

LET US PROVIDE YOU WITH THE INFORMATION NECESSARY FOR YOU TO MAKE AN INFORMED DECISION TO COMMIT YOURSELF TO THE BAPTISM PROCESS SO THAT YOU AND YOUR FAMILY CAN CELEBRATE THIS LIFE-CHANGING EVENT TOGETHER. CONTACT US FOR MORE INFORMATION ONCE YOU ARE READY TO BE WASHED IN THE WATER THAT REPRESENTS THE BLOOD OF THE LAMB!

THE START OF THE PROCESS TOWARD SALVATION IS BAPTISM

JESUS EXPLAINED IT TO NICODEMUS AND ACTS 2:38 HAS THE DETAIL.

Picture of your Baptism

CHURCH WEB ADDRESS

NEW MEMBER PACKET
TEMPLATE
Location
8.5 x 11 landscape
Download the Pagemaker & PDF file to use as a template at:
www.LessonsForLifeBooks.com/templates/NewMembers.zip

LOCATION

CHURCH NAME IS LOCATED AT CHURCH ADDRESS - CITY, STATE ZIP.

CHURCH PHONE NUMBER

Map to Church Location

SINCE WE BEGAN IN YEAR
CHURCH NAME IS EXPERIENCING
STEADY GROWTH

Picture of Your Church
or Office, etc

CHURCH WEB ADDRESS

NEW MEMBER PACKET
TEMPLATE
Evangelism
8.5 x 11 landscape
Download the Pagemaker & PDF file to use as a template at:
www.LessonsForLifeBooks.com/templates/NewMembers.zip

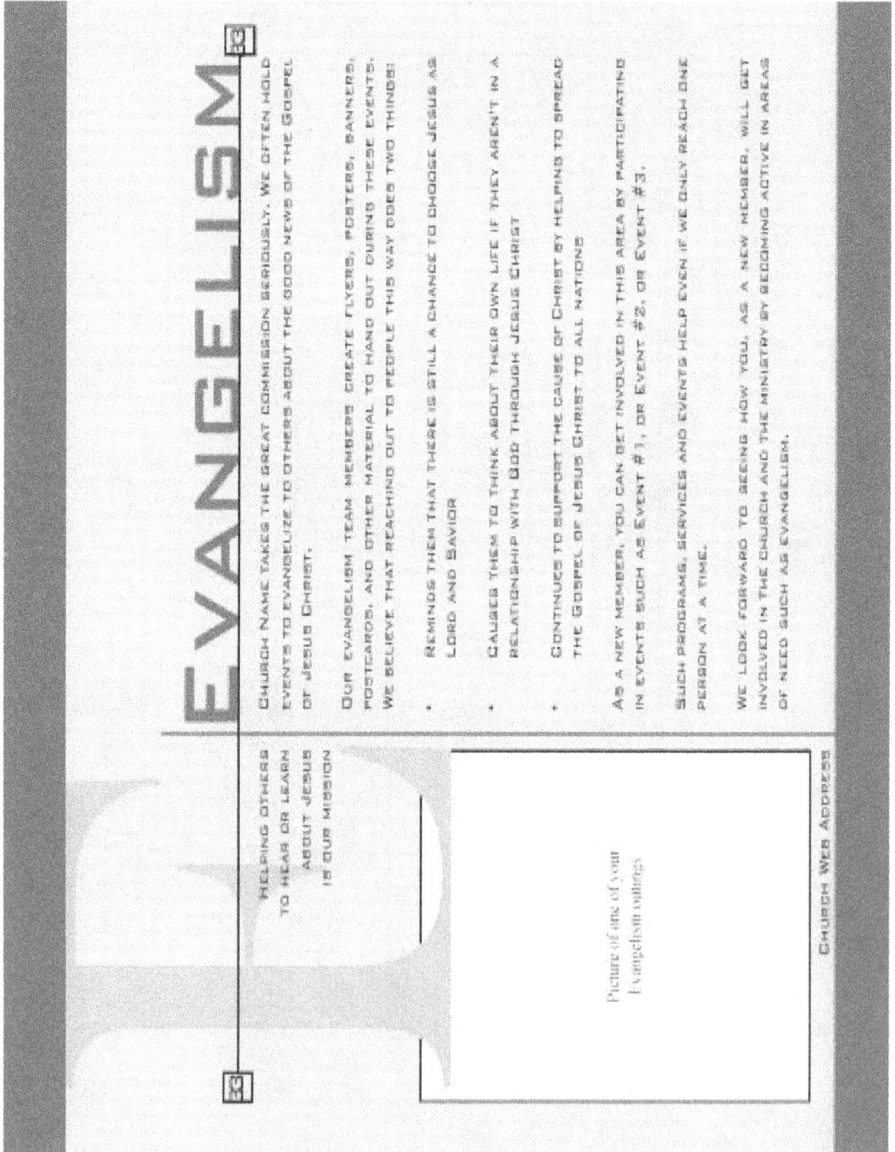

NEW MEMBER PACKET
TEMPLATE
Topics For Study
8.5 x 11 landscape
Download the Pagemaker & PDF file to use as a template at:
www.LessonsForLifeBooks.com/templates/NewMembers.zip

TOPICS FOR STUDY

TOPIC 1

WORD OF GOD

JOHN 1:1- TELLS US "IN THE BEGINNING WAS THE WORD, THE WORD WAS WITH GOD AND THE WORD WAS GOD." SO GOD IS HIS WORD. WE BELIEVE IT IS TRUE IN ITS ENTIRETY. THE BIBLE IS IN ESSENCE THE MIND OF GOD. IT IS WHO GOD IS AND WHAT GOD IS ALL ABOUT. YOU CAN NOT SEPARATE GOD FROM HIS WORD. IF YOU WANT TO KNOW GOD, YOU MUST KNOW HIS WORD. THE BIBLE IS THE INSPIRED WORD OF GOD WRITTEN BY THE HANDS OF MEN AS GOD DIRECTED THEM. (II TIM. 3:16)

TOPIC 2

JESUS CHRIST, HUMAN AND DIVINE

JESUS CHRIST IS THE SON OF GOD AND HE ALSO IS GOD IN THE FLESH. HE WAS BOTH HUMAN AND DIVINE. (I TIM. 3:16)- TELL US "GREAT IS THE MYSTERY OF GODLINESS: GOD WAS MANIFEST IN THE FLESH..." MANIFEST MEANS TO BE MADE FLESH, IN OTHER WORDS, GOD WHO IS A SPIRIT WAS MADE FLESH IN THE PERSON OF JESUS CHRIST AND WAS BORN OF A VIRGIN, DWELT ON EARTH, DIED FOR OUR SINS, RESURRECTED HIMSELF IN 3 DAYS, AND ASCENDED BACK INTO HEAVEN. (ST.JOHN 1 4:7-9)

TOPIC 3

HOLY (SPIRIT) GHOST

THE HOLY GHOST IS THE SPIRIT OF GOD THAT COMES TO GIVE US POWER TO LIVE HOLY (ACTS 1:8). WHEN YOU RECEIVE THE HOLY GHOST, YOU WILL SPEAK IN OTHER TONGUES AS THE SPIRIT EMPOWERS YOU (ACTS 1:4). THE HOLY GHOST IS FOR EVERYONE (ACTS 2:39). AND YOU MUST HAVE IN ORDER TO MAKE IT TO HEAVEN. (ST. JOHN 3:5) YOU CAN RECEIVE THE HOLY GHOST BY REPENTING AND BEING SINCERE IN YOUR HEART AND ASK GOD TO GIVE YOU HIS HOLY SPIRIT, AND HE WILL. YOU WILL BEGIN TO HEAR YOURSELF SPEAK IN TONGUES (A DIFFERENT LANGUAGE) AND YOU WON'T UNDERSTAND WHAT YOU ARE SAYING, BECAUSE YOU ARE SPEAKING DIRECTLY TO GOD IN HIS HEAVENLY LANGUAGE (I COR. 14:2) (ACTS 10:44-46) (ACTS 19:1-6)

PLEASE FEEL FREE TO TALK TO PASTOR NAME FIRST LADY NAME, IF YOU NEED OR THINK YOU NEED THE HOLY GHOST AND THEY WILL BE MORE THAN HAPPY TO WORK WITH YOU TO RECEIVE THE HOLY GHOST. ALSO YOU CAN COME UP DURING ANY OF THE CHURCH ALTAR CALL (AT THE END OF THE PREACHING) TO RECEIVE THE HOLY SPIRIT.

CHURCH WEB ADDRESS

NEW MEMBER PACKET
TEMPLATE
Topics For Study
8.5 x 11 landscape
Download the Pagemaker & PDF file to use as a template at:
www.LessonsForLifeBooks.com/templates/NewMembers.zip

TOPICS FOR STUDY

TOPIC 4

REPENTANCE

THE PURPOSE OF REPENTANCE IS TO BE GODLY SORRY AND TURN FROM YOUR WICKED AND SINNING WAYS. GOD WILL ACCEPT YOUR REPENTANCE WHEN YOU ARE SINCERE FROM YOUR HEART. REPENTANCE IS ONE OF THE FIRST STEPS TO BECOMING SAVED. (ACTS 2:38), (ST.MARK 1:15) (I JOHN 1:9)

TOPIC 5

WATER BAPTISM IN JESUS NAME

WE BAPTIZE BY IMMERSION, TAKING A PERSON UNDER WATER VERY QUICKLY, JUST AS JESUS WAS BAPTIZED BY JOHN THE BAPTIST. JESUS TOLD NICODEMUS, "YOU MUST BE BORN OF THE WATER AND OF THE SPIRIT. THE PURPOSE OF WATER BAPTISM IN JESUS NAME IS TO CLEANSE AND REMOVE (REMISSION) YOUR SINS (ACTS 2:38). DURING ALTAR CALL, YOU CAN COME UP TO BE BAPTIZE IN JESUS NAME AND WE WILL ARRANGE AT A LATER TIME TO BAPTIZE YOU IN JESUS NAME. (ACTS 10:47-48), (EPH. 4:5)

TOPIC 6

IMPORTANCE OF PRAYER

PRAYER IS ONE OF THE MOST POWERFUL WEAPONS WE HAVE. WHEN YOU PRAY GOD IS NOT CONCERNED ABOUT HOW ARTICULATE YOU SPEAK. HE JUST WANTS TO HEAR WHAT IS ON YOUR MIND AND HEART. PRAYER BUILDS UP YOUR RELATIONSHIP WITH GOD AND IT BRINGS YOU CLOSER TO GOD THE MORE TIME YOU SPEND WITH HIM IN PRAYER. IF YOU WILL HUMBLE YOURSELF AND PRAY GOD WILL BLESS YOU, YOUR FAMILY, FRIENDS, AND EVEN OUR WORLD (II CHRONICLES 7:14).

PRAYER SHOULD BE A PART OF YOUR DAILY LIFE. YOU SHOULD SET ASIDE CERTAIN TIMES TO PRAY EVERYDAY. IN OTHER WORDS, MAKE YOURSELF A DAILY PRAYER SCHEDULE AND PRAY AT THOSE CERTAIN TIMES. IF YOU ARE NOT USED TO PRAYING, START OFF SMALL AND PROGRESS AS YOU BECOME MORE ACCUSTOMED TO PRAYING. EXAMPLE: YOU COULD START OFF BY PRAYING 5 MINUTES IN THE MORNING, 5 MINUTES ON YOUR LUNCH BREAK OR NOON, AND 5 MINUTES BEFORE YOU GO TO SLEEP AT NIGHT. THIS IS ONLY 15 MINUTES A DAY. IF YOU ARE ALREADY USED TO PRAYING TRY 15 OR 30 MINUTES THREE TIMES A DAY. (LUKE 6:12) (ACTS 3:1) (MARK 1:35).

READ: PSALM 5:3

CHURCH WEB ADDRESS

NEW MEMBER PACKET
TEMPLATE
Topics For Study
8.5 x 11 landscape
Download the Pagemaker & PDF file to use as a template at:
www.LessonsForLifeBooks.com/templates/NewMembers.zip

TOPICS FOR STUDY

TOPIC 7

FASTING

FASTING IS SETTING ASIDE TIME IN WHICH ABSTAIN FROM FOOD, WATER, AND/OR OTHER THINGS THAT OUR FLESH LOVES TO DO. FASTING BRINGS YOUR BODY (FLESH) UNDER CONTROL, SO THAT YOUR SPIRITUAL MAN (PERSON) CAN TAKE CONTROL. FASTING STRENGTHENS YOU SPIRITUALLY. (MATT. 6:16-18) (MATT. 17:21) WE DO NOT EAT ANY FOOD DURING A FAST, BUT IT IS OK TO DRINK WATER. YOU DON'T HAVE TO FAST AT ANY PARTICULAR TIME) YOU CAN CHOOSE ANY DAY AND TIME. ALSO YOU SHOULD SET ASIDE SOME TIME TO PRAY, AND READ YOUR BIBLE, IF YOU ARE AT WORK OR SCHOOL, YOU COULD USE YOUR BREAK TIME. FASTING KEEPS US REMINDED TO SACRIFICE AS INDIVIDUALS, AND AS A CHURCH. I ENCOURAGE EVERYONE TO GET ASIDE TIMES FOR FASTING. IF IT'S YOUR FIRST TIME, YOU CAN EVEN ASK SOMEONE TO FAST WITH YOU.

TOPIC 8

FAITH

FAITH IS VERY IMPORTANT TO GOD (HEB. 11:6). BECAUSE FAITH IS BELIEVING IN SOMETHING YOU CANNOT SEE, FEEL, AND TOUCH IT (HEB. 11:1). YOUR FAITH SHOWS GOD THAT YOU ARE PUTTING YOUR TRUST IN HIM AND NOT IN YOURSELF OR SOMEONE ELSE. YOU MUST HAVE FAITH IN ORDER FOR GOD TO ANSWER YOUR PRAYERS. WHATEVER YOU ASK GOD FOR YOU MUST BELIEVE THAT HE WILL DO IT FOR YOU EVEN BEFORE YOU PRAY. ALL SAINTS MUST HAVE FAITH IN GOD. IT IS A REQUIREMENT. ST. MARK 9:23

TOPIC 9

ABSTAIN FROM SIN

SIN IS WHEN YOU TRANSGRESS OR DISOBEY THE WORD OF GOD (1 JOHN 3:4). SIN SEPARATES YOU FROM GOD AND WHEN YOU SIN YOU MUST BE QUICK TO REPENT AND BE WILLING TO STAY AWAY THAT WHICH CAUSED YOU TO SIN. FORNICATION IS HAVING SEX WITH SOMEONE YOU ARE NOT MARRIED TO. THIS IS SIN, ACCORDING TO THE BIBLE. SHACKING USUALLY LEADS TO FORNICATION, THEREFORE IF YOU ARE NOT MARRIED, YOU SHOULD NOT BE LIVING TOGETHER. SHACKING IS WHEN A COUPLE WHO IS NOT MARRIED BUT LIVING TOGETHER. WHEN YOU FORNICATE, YOU ARE SINNING AGAINST YOUR BODY. THE DIFFERENCE BETWEEN SAINTS AND SINNERS IS THAT SAINTS PRACTICE LIVING HOLY AND ACCORDING TO THE WORD OF GOD. DO YOUR VERY BEST TO STAY AWAY FROM ANYONE OR ANYTHING THAT CAUSES YOU TO SIN.

CHURCH WEB ADDRESS

NEW MEMBER PACKET
TEMPLATE
Topics For Study

8.5 x 11 landscape

Download the Pagemaker & PDF file to use as a template at:
www.LessonsForLifeBooks.com/templates/NewMembers.zip

TOPICS FOR STUDY

TOPIC 9 ...CONTINUED

THERE ARE MANY WAYS TO SIN LYING, GOSSIP, BACKBITE, JEALOUSY, MURDER, HATRED, ENVY, LUST, UNFORGIVENESS, ADULTERY, FORNICATION, SMOKING CIGARETTES, DOING DRUGS, ALCOHOL. YOUR BODY IS THE TEMPLE OF THE HOLY GHOST. DO NOT DEFILE IT. YOU CAN ALWAYS FEEL FREE TO MAKE AN APPOINTMENT WITH PASTOR NAME TO CONFESS YOUR SINS. (II COR.6:13-20), (I JOHN 1:9)

TOPIC 10 — HEALINGS AND MIRACLES

WE BELIEVE IN DIVINE HEALING AND MIRACLES THROUGH PRAYER AND LAYING ON OF HANDS IN JESUS NAME (MARK 16:17-18). WE HAVE HEALING AND DELIVERANCE SERVICES HERE AT CHURCH NAME. WE HAVE HAD PEOPLE WHO TESTIFIED HERE ABOUT THE MIRACLES AND HEALINGS THEY HAVE EXPERIENCED WHILE IN OUR SERVICES THROUGH THE POWER OF GOD. THIS IS A CHURCH OF MIRACLES AND BLESSINGS OF ALL KINDS WHERE THE ANOINTING POWER OF GOD IS AT WORK!!! ST. LUKE 10:19

TOPIC 11 — TRUTH ABOUT HEAVEN AND HELL

THERE IS A HEAVEN AND A HELL. HEAVEN IS RESERVED FOR THE RIGHTEOUS, THOSE WHO HAVE PREPARED THEMSELVES FOR GOD BY LIVING HOLY ACCORDING TO HIS WORD. HELL WAS PREPARED FOR THE DEVIL AND THE FALLEN ANGELS THAT TRIED TO OVERTHROW GOD IN HEAVEN, BUT THOSE WHO DO NOT LIVE ACCORDING TO THE WORD OF GOD WILL BE SENT TO HELL (LUKE 16:22-23) (REV. CHAPTER 20)

TOPIC 12 — TITHES AND OFFERINGS - KEYS TO BLESSINGS

EVERYONE SHOULD PAY THEIR TITHES AND GIVE AN OFFERING. YOUR TITHES IS 10% OF YOUR INCREASE THAT INCLUDE MONEY THAT YOU EARN FROM WORKING AND MONEY YOU GET WHEN SOMEONE BLESSES YOU (AN INCOME) ALSO. THE BIBLE SAYS YOU WILL BE CURSED WITH A CURSE, IF YOU DO NOT PAY YOUR TITHES (MALACHI 3:9). BUT IF YOU PAY YOUR TITHES AND OFFERINGS YOU WILL BE BLESSED, BECAUSE GOD SAID HE WILL OPEN UP THE WINDOWS OF HEAVEN AND POUR YOU OUT A BLESSING THAT YOU WON'T HAVE ROOM ENOUGH TO RECEIVE IT (MALACHI 3:10). MAL. 3:8-10, II COR. 9:6-7 GIVING IS YOUR KEY TO BEING BLESSED. LUKE 6:38 TELL US TO "GIVE AND IT SHALL BE GIVEN UNTO YOU."

CHURCH Web Address

NEW MEMBER PACKET
TEMPLATE
List Of Ministries
8.5 x 11 landscape
Download the Pagemaker & PDF file to use as a template at:
www.LessonsForLifeBooks.com/templates/NewMembers.zip

LIST OF MINISTRIES

DETAILED

MINISTRY OF ARTS

MINISTRY NAME
CHAIRPERSON NAME

MINISTRY NAME
CHAIRPERSON NAME

MINISTRY NAME
CHAIRPERSON NAME

MINISTRY NAME
CHAIRPERSON NAME

MINISTRY NAME
CHAIRPERSON NAME

MINISTRY NAME
CHAIRPERSON NAME

MINISTRY NAME
CHAIRPERSON NAME

MINISTRY NAME
CHAIRPERSON NAME

CHURCH NAME CORE MINISTRIES

MEN .... CHAIRMAN
WOMEN .... CHAIRPERSON
YOUTH .... CHAIRPERSON
USHER .... CHAIRPERSON
PRAYER TEAM .... CHAIRPERSON
EVANGELISM .... CHAIRPERSON
NURSING HOME MINISTRY .... CHAIRPERSON
NEW MEMBERS .... CHAIRPERSON
PUBLIC RELATIONS .... CHAIRPERSON
ALTAR WORKERS .... CHAIRPERSON
BAPTISM .... CHAIRPERSON
PASTOR AIDE .... CHAIRPERSON
BIBLE SCHOOL PRESIDENT .... CHAIRPERSON
OUTREACH .... CHAIRPERSON
CHURCH FUNDRAISER .... CHAIRPERSON
CHILDREN'S CHOIR .... CHAIRPERSON
YOUTH CHOIR .... CHAIRPERSON
MASS CHOIR .... CHAIRPERSON
SINGLE MOTHERS .... CHAIRPERSON
SINGLE WOMEN .... CHAIRPERSON
FINANCE .... CHAIRPERSON
FOREIGN MISSION .... CHAIRPERSON
MARRIED COUPLES .... CHAIRPERSON

CHURCH NAME YOUTH MINISTRIES

YOUTH MINISTRY NAME .... CHAIRPERSON
YOUTH MINISTRY NAME .... CHAIRPERSON
YOUTH MINISTRY NAME .... CHAIRPERSON

CHURCH WEB ADDRESS

NEW MEMBER PACKET
TEMPLATE
List Of Ministries
8.5 x 11 landscape
Download the Pagemaker & PDF file to use as a template at:
www.LessonsForLifeBooks.com/templates/NewMembers.zip

DETAILED LIST OF MINISTRIES

MINISTRY OF MUSIC
Head Musician .... HEAD MUSICIAN NAME
Co-Head Musician .... CO-HEAD MUSICIAN NAME
Organist .... ORGANIST NAME

CHURCH NAME MINISTRY OF INFORMATION
Newsletter Editor/Design .... CHAIRPERSON
Video Engineer .... CHAIRPERSON
TV Ministry .... CHAIRPERSON
Website Admin/Design .... CHAIRPERSON

CHURCH NAME MINISTRY OF COUNSELING
Confession Of Sins .... CONTACT THE PASTOR ONLY
Marriage Counseling .... CONTACT THE PASTOR OR FIRST LADY
Family Counseling .... CONTACT THE PASTOR OR FIRST LADY
How To Become A New Member .... CHAIRPERSON
Christian Counseling .... CONTACT THE PASTOR OR FIRST LADY
How To Be Saved .... CONTACT THE PASTOR OR FIRST LADY

All Other Counseling Matters .... CONTACT THE PASTOR

CHURCH NAME ADDITIONAL INFO
Church Secretary .... CHURCH SECRETARY NAME
Phone
Email

Hours:
Monday - Friday
9am to 5pm

Church Web Address

NEW MEMBER PACKET
TEMPLATE
Rear Cover
8.5 x 11 landscape
Download the Pagemaker & PDF file to use as a template at:
www.LessonsForLifeBooks.com/templates/NewMembers.zip

GENERAL INFORMATION

40

CONTACTS

CHURCH NAME

CHURCH OFFICE .... PHONE NUMBER
CHURCH FAX .... FAX NUMBER
CHURCH WEBSITE .... WEB ADDRESS
EMERGENCY CELL .... EMERGENCY CELL NUMBER
(FOR EMERGENCIES & MEMBERS ONLY!)

MAILING

CHURCH NAME
ADDRESS
CITY, STATE, ZIP

PHOTO/LOGO

Church Logo

40

What's Next

Now that you've read, and seen, from my experiences, the process of creating dynamic and effective New Member's Packets, let's discuss taking your efforts to another level. While reading this book, if the thought of going digital with this project by creating a 'New Members DVD' let me be the first to say it is easily possible. How? Simple. By taking the content from the template in this book, and using it to lay out a storyline in video editing software. I've done it half dozen times for churches and their new members have truly enjoyed the experience of having the visual edition of the New Member Packet.

So, think about it. And once you've made the decision to go digital, email me at: GoDigital@LessonsForLifeBooks.com and I'll do my very best to make time to assist in any way I can, including providing a template you can use to do it.

Section Four
BONUS SECTION - New Members DVD

Going Digital

So, what would going digital with your New Members Packet actually look like? Let me tell you that the word 'Amazing' doesn't even describe it. I mean, think about it, if you were a new member, would you rather read about you new church's choirs in a 40-page packet, or actually be able to watch clips of the various choirs using their gifts to lift their voices in praise to God through songs of worship, on a DVD player, in the comfort of my own home?

For me, it's an easy choice. I would choose digital every time. But I'm a visual person. As you can probably tell by the number of books God has inspired me to write that have 'visual' tips and pointers. And I understand the tremendous impact that a DVD can have versus paragraphs in a packet. I say all this to encourage you to create the New Member Packet in printed form because it's a great for use in your New Member Class.

Going Digital Reminder: Putting together a digital version of your church's New Member Packet takes a bit more than just typing, placing graphics on a page, and printing the final draft. It takes an even greater commitment from someone to learn, or use skills they already have, to gather, lay out and edit video into a dynamic visual presentation that can be seen on DVD.

But I also make the push for you to consider **going digital** as well, because both can make a considerable, measurable and significant difference in how your new members achieve their goal of learning about, getting comfortable with, and finding a place to fit into your church when they join.

Going digital, in addition to a print version of you New Member Packet, I believe, will have an even bigger influence on a new members whose looking for a forward-thinking, progressive church, rather than one that will not embrace technology, social media, and other mediums, as a way to reach the lost.

Going Digital

WHERE TO START

So where on Earth would you start the process of Going Digital with your New Member Packet? The answer is simple: "Your New Member Packet". Let me explain...

All the content that you plan to gather for the printed version of your New Member Packet, can be used for the DVD version, especially the videos and pictures.

Again, if you make the decision to go digital, I'll do my very best to assist you in any way I can. But, in the interim, I'll include a few screenshots of the software and process I use to help you understand how with just a few tools, you can easily turn your printed packet, into digital dynamics! [HINT: The 'pc' software I use for video editing is available at avs4you.com]

SCREEN SAMPLE:

The 'pc' video editing software that I use to edit many types of projects, operates on timelines and transitions, effects and overlays, and can help you in your project as well.

Getting Started Tip:
If you haven't already, just like you assigned the print version of your awesome New Member Packet to someone, assign creation of the digital version as well. Using these tools to teach your New Member's Class can help enhance your 'first impression' presentation to your new members, and put two valuable resources in the hands of your teachers.

Going Digital

LAYOUT

Once you have the 'pc' version of the software I use, to start your projects, I recommend setting up the following storyboard so you can follow a structured layout and get your DVD done without much effort.

Section One

| Welcome from your Pastor | [video] |
| Welcome from your First Lady | [video] |

Section Two thru End

Again, your DVD should be an exact duplicate of the contents of the printed version of your New Members Packet. Keeping it this way, will make it much easier for whoever teaches your New Members Class to have students follow along in the packet while watching the DVD. Both tools, can provide a dynamic foundation for presenting your church.

Going Digital Reminder: Putting together a digital version of your church's New Member Packet takes a bit more than just typing, placing graphics on a page, and printing the final draft. It takes an even greater commitment from someone to learn, or use skills they already have, to gather, lay out and edit video into a dynamic visual presentation that can be seen on DVD.

SCREEN SAMPLE:

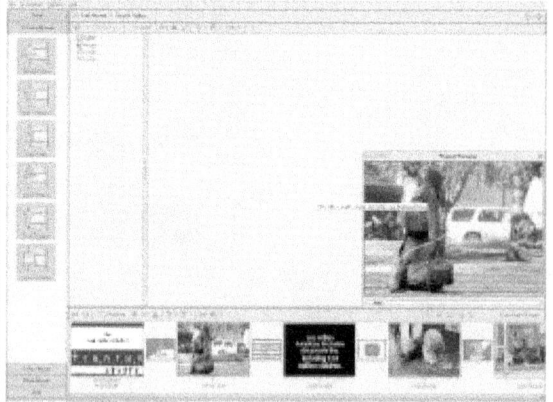

The 'pc' video editing software that I use to edit many types of projects, operates on timelines and transitions, effects and overlays, and can help you in your project as well.

Going Digital

AUDIO

The way I do audio is by using another software, [HINT: which you can find at www.naturalreaders.com] that can easily help you create the audio files needed to help your New Member DVD transition from section to section using the guided audio of narrated voice over.

Using voiceover, I include my own instrumental background music, which also incorporate parts of sermons, choir songs, and other relevant items.

However you do your audio, using the video editing software makes it easy to sync your audio clips, with voice over narrative, to your video clips. Again, IF you need assistance, I'm happy to help when and where I'm able. God did not give me all these gifts, skills, talents, abilities, memory, knowledge, and resources to keep to myself, for myself. So email me.

SCREEN SAMPLE:

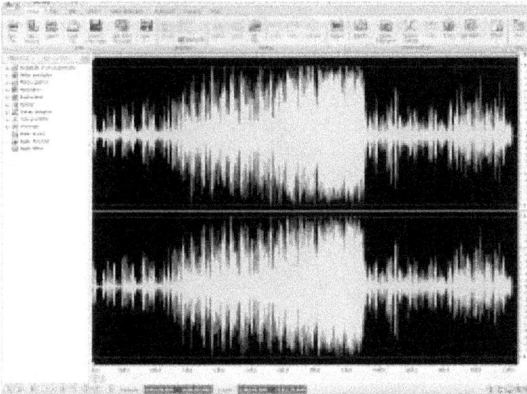

Synching audio with your video is easy using the video editing software I use. I know about one other 'mac' version, which I also use, but is much more expensive than the 'pc' version.

Going Digital Reminder: Wherever your church has had worship services, and a video camera has been present, you have 'audio'. How? Simple. There is video on the camera, yes, but you can also 'strip' out the audio for use as voice-overs when needed. Be creative, let God use you, and you will be surprised at what you can accomplish when you put forth a little effort. [Prov. 16:3]

Going Digital

VIDEO & PICTURES

In almost every page of the 'Content' section of this book, I reiterate how important it is to use pictures and video when able, to give new members a visual picture of your church.

Using narrative by itself is fine if you can't do any better, but if you can make the effort to take the time to collect and gather as many pictures and videos from your past and present members phones, cameras, etc., it will prove to be beyond beneficial in the long-run and you will be more than glad you did.

Reminder: If a picture is worth a thousand words, then how much is a video? The answer: priceless. This is not the Great Commission, nor am I the Great Commander, but I'll use one word from it, "GO." Get to work.

Going Digital Reminder: Software applications are just tools to use to help get the job done. The real work is in 'you.' Whatever you put into your New Member Packet, your New Member DVD, and your New Member Class, is what you're going to get out of it. Remember, plant, someone else will water, and God will give the increase. Don't try to do it all, just do your part.

SCREEN SAMPLE:

Once the video editing project is completed, and the file is ready to be split into chapters, although the video editor is quite capable, I use another software to output the file to DVD.

Going Digital

EFFECTS, ETC.

You don't need to be a graphic designer, commercial artists, or any sort of expert in desktop publishing to make your New Member Packet, or New Member DVD come alive with rich and exciting visual effects.

Within each of the software applications are plenty of templates ready to use for transitions, moving text, gradients, and all types of other cool effects.

Once you're committed to the project, and you've committed the project to God, He will order your steps and direct your paths [Proverbs 16:3].

There is no greater reward than to allow God through His Holy spirit to lead, guide, and direct you through a project that uplifts His Church.

SCREEN SAMPLE:

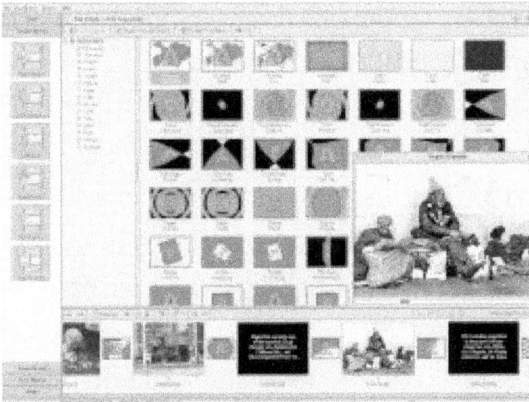

Effect and transitions are ready and waiting inside each of the software applications I use for video editing, audio editing, and final output. You can use any one, but choose wisely.

Going Digital Reminder: Wherever your church has had worship services, and a video camera has been present, you have 'audio'. How? Simple. There is video on the camera, yes, but you can also 'strip' out the audio for use as voice-overs when needed. Be creative, let God use you, and you will be surprised at what you can accomplish when you put forth a little effort. [Prov. 16:3]

Thank You

I've written over 80 books to date. This Ministry has been a tremendous Blessing in my life, and I'm grateful to God for His redemption, reuse, restoration, and reclamation, as my life many years before this was nothing more than a reckless shell of a man.

I'm including this note of thanks to all the readers of this book, whether you're a pastor, or the layleader assigned to the task of creating a New Member Packet.

I thank you because you have the insight of how vitally important new members are to any church, and thank you for taking time to recognize what God has shown me over many years.

Without new members, churches would eventually cease to operate.

Template Reminder:
The 40-page template was designed to showcase these words:

WITH
GOD
ALL
THINGS
ARE
POSSIBLE

Start at page 60 of this printed version, end at page 86. God Bless!

I'm also including a note of thanks for those who are tasked with designing and developing your New Member's Packet.

I thank you because without you allowing your gifts, skills, talents, abilities, memory, knowledge, resources, and willingness to used in this process, it may have never been done.

Lastly, if you ever need assistance in making this process happen in your church, feel free to email me. Go to the Contact Page on the website:
LessonsForLifeBooks.com
...it will eventually make it to my desk.

Contact

Author: Keith Hammond
President
Lessons For Life Books, Inc.
7455 France Avenue South #305
Edina, MN 55435

(952) 884-5498 ofc
(952) 884-3785 fax

author@LessonsForLifeBooks.com

web: LessonsForLifeBooks.com

How to Find Us:

Google:
'keith hammond lessons for life books'

Barnes & Noble:
bn.com
'keith hammond'

Bookwire.com
'keith hammond'

Amazon:
'keith hammond' or 'book title'

Kindle:
coming soon

Catalog Reminder:
The best way to get an overall view of the more than 80 books I've written, is to download the full-color, interactive catalog from our website.

LessonsForLifeBooks.com/catalog.html

Every book page has a link to the preview of that book, and includes ISBN info, ordering info, etc.

NEW MEMBERS = NEW GROWTH
It's up to you how you nurture them.

Lessons For Life Books

PUBLISHERS

L E S S O N S F O R L I F E B O O K S . C O M

www.ingramcontent.com/pod-product-compliance
Lightning Source LLC
Chambersburg PA
CBHW052140090426
42741CB00009B/2161